25 KIDS
WHO CHANGED
WORLD HISTORY

SHORT, INSPIRING BIOGRAPHIES FROM OUTSIDE THE U.S. WITH ILLUSTRATIONS AND DISCUSSION GUIDES FOR YOUNG READERS

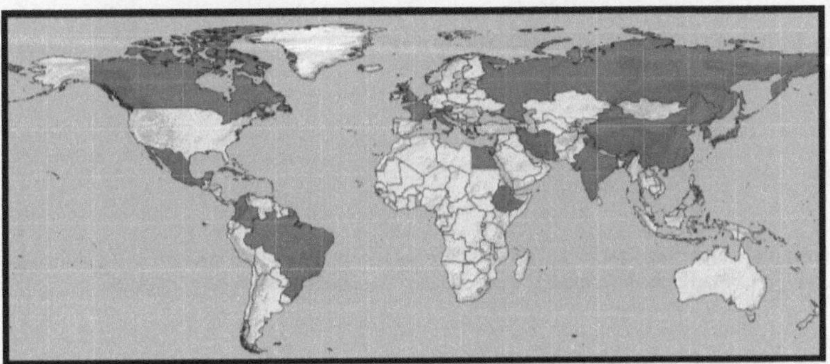

N. H. GREENWOOD

SAGE VI PRESS

Copyright © 2026 by N. H. Greenwood

All rights reserved.

Published by Sage VI Press. The Historic 25™ is a trademark of Visage Advisors LLC.

The content contained within this book may not be reproduced, duplicated or transmitted without direct written permission from the author or the publisher.

Under no circumstances will any blame or legal responsibility be held against the publisher, or author, for any damages, reparation, or monetary loss due to the information contained within this book. Either directly or indirectly. You are responsible for your own choices, actions, and results.

"HISTORY TEACHES EVERYTHING, EVEN THE FUTURE."

– ALPHONSE DE LAMARTINE, FRENCH POET

Contents

*O*n May 7, 1429, *deadly arrows were flying everywhere as 17-year-old Joan rode her horse bravely into battle. Joan could barely hear her own voice over the pounding hoofbeats and the clang of swords on armor. She yelled as loud as she could, urging her fellow French soldiers to keep going. Then it happened: whizz... THUD! And then PAIN. An arrow had struck her above the chest, right where she'd warned it would. She cried. Who wouldn't? And everyone thought, That's it. She's done.*

But they shouldn't have doubted Joan of Arc. She came back to the battlefield that same day. Legend says she pulled the arrow out herself! Then Joan inspired France to victory.

I wrote this book to tell true stories like Joan's. Just a teenager, she became a symbol of France's strength. You may have heard of Joan of Arc, but do you really know her story? In these pages, you'll get to read it! And you'll learn about other courageous kids from all across the world and across centuries. Historic kids who worked hard, fought bravely and stood up for things even when it wasn't easy. Kids who were not so different from you!

What's in this Book. The 25 chapters of this book span five continents and more than 500 years of history. Each chapter includes a short, fun biography followed by review questions to check some facts and then discussion questions. Many of my readers tell me that the discussion questions are their favorite part — they give them a chance to think about the story and what it means in their lives. I wrote those questions to encourage conversation — no right or wrong answers!

Each chapter also has illustrations to help you picture what's happening. They're not meant to be exact re-creations of the moment but to give you an idea and to bring the characters to life. There's also a project idea in each chapter if you really want to dive into history. Those projects help make this book a better tool for teaching or for families on rainy days.

The book is set up alphabetically by country. Within a country, the kids are ordered by time. Note that the countries are named the way we generally refer to them when studying history in the United States. For example, while North Korea and South Korea are now independent nations, the biography from Korea is listed under the historical "Korea."

Also, you'll notice that Hawaii (spelled Hawai'i in the Hawaiian language) is listed on its own — that's because most of that story takes place when Hawaii was an independent kingdom, before it became a U.S. territory, and later a state.

A small map is at the start of every chapter. The country for the chapter is shaded in the map.

Historical Context. Each chapter pulls from a time and place in history. No matter where you're from, most of the chapters will take place somewhere else — there are 19 countries in here! I included enough historical background in each story so you could understand better how and why things happened the way they did. I tried to limit the number of extra facts so you wouldn't get too bogged down in a million new things, but there's still plenty to learn.

You'll get to know really cool stuff you might not know right now: the fall of the Chinese emperors, Colombia's struggle for independence, life on the Canadian frontier, Ethiopia's wars with Italy, and much more. I also tried to show how to pronounce certain words — I think it stinks to read something to yourself and not know how to say it. So hopefully that helps! There's also a glossary at the end of the book with definitions of key words and names.

Who are the 25 Kids. I chose boys and girls from all kinds of different backgrounds and places and times outside the U.S. I wanted to be sure that the subjects had done something important before turning 20. I looked for people who had actually made an impact as teens or younger, not just prepared to blaze trails later. I also wanted to stay away from kids who were given a big role early in life but didn't really do much until later. I didn't want a book full of 5-year-old kings who were waiting around while adults made the decisions. There *are* some young royals in here, but their stories are awesome and chosen carefully.

Now, you could say that some of the kids are a little old, like Mary Shelley, who published her book, *Frankenstein*, at 20. But she wrote the book at 19. And yes, lots of kids grew up faster in historic times, but I included kids whose feats were special anyway. In Shelley's case, writing a groundbreaking novel was incredible for a teenager. And honestly, that might be my favorite chapter in this book.

Lastly, I sought to include something for everyone. There are queens, kings, soldiers, an artist, a math whiz, a writer, a scientist, a healer, a soccer player, musicians, inventors (and a musician-inventor!) and more. These are short, story-driven biographies focused on what each kid did and why it mattered. The goals are simply to discover these amazing kids, to get excited about history and to be inspired! The lessons of courage, hard work, loyalty, charity and service are hopefully timeless. Every reader can find someone to like in here.

About the Author. I'm N.H. Greenwood, and this is my fourth book, the second in this series about *The Historic 25*. My first book, *25 Kids Who Changed American History*, got a great response. Readers told me they liked the variety, and they wanted more. So I set out to find more variety of incredible young people and learned a lot along the way. I have an Ivy League history degree, three kids, and I grew up in a house built around 1730, which is old even *outside* the U.S. So history has been all around me my whole life, especially as a kid when the winter came through the walls! I'm so excited to share this broader, older world history with you! I hope it makes you think deeper and dream bigger!

About You. We all come from somewhere and, before that, from somewhere else. Thinking back to Joan of Arc, you may have family from France. You probably know someone with ties to France. Or you may want to visit there someday. This book will take you to France and Europe. It will also bring you to America's neighbors in North and South

America, to Africa, the Middle East, South and East Asia and the Pacific. In this book you might walk in the footsteps of your ancestors.

As the world gets smaller, there's much to learn about what shaped the ideas of people all over. As you read, ask yourself, *if I grew up where this happened, how would this make me feel*? How is history different across places and time? How is it the same? What is different from what you expected? More on all that at the end of the book...

Now before you turn the page, kindly do me one small favor. Take a look at the table of contents and start with the story you're most excited about. Someone you've heard of? A place you've been? A place you want to go? That's one great thing about this book — you don't have to read it in order!

So get ready to go on an adventure through time. You're going to love some of these kids. I know I did. As you read, think about what you like to do and how these stories might inspire you to do something special, to make a difference. Your own history awaits. The world awaits!

CHAPTER 1

AUSTRIA: WOLFGANG AMADEUS MOZART (1756-1791)

A BOY WHO PLAYED FOR KINGS

This little boy was so talented at just six years old that he was brought to the royal court to play music for the Austrian empress. This was a very special kid with big dreams and a big personality. Indeed, at one point, when he slipped and fell at the palace, a young princess helped him up. He told the older girl, "I will marry you!" He did not end up marrying the princess (in fact, she went on to become queen of France!). But this spirited boy did become one of the greatest musical composers in history. This is the story of Wolfgang Amadeus Mozart.

The Mozart house in Salzburg, Austria, was always full of music. As a young boy, Wolfgang watched while his older sister learned to play a clavichord, an instrument with keys like a piano. Little Wolfie's father, Leopold, was a violinist and music teacher, and he taught Wolfie's sister how to play. But he couldn't keep Wolfie away from the keys, and the Mozart boy started to play the clavichord at just three years old! By the time he was five, he was already playing from his sister's songbooks. He had an incredible natural gift. He could play a song the first time he saw the music.

When Wolfie was about six, his father's friend came to visit They looked in on Wolfie, who was drawing on paper. When they asked what he was doing, Wolfie showed them that he was composing music. The writing was messy, and the men laughed — it looked hard to play, maybe too hard. But Wolfie explained that it "must be practiced before it can be performed." Hello?! Of course! And then Wolfie played a bit of his music. His dad's eyes filled with tears — the messy writing was in fact lovely music! Wolfgang was a *prodigy*, a young child with awesome talent and the skill of an expert adult.

Leopold stopped teaching others so that he could focus on his gifted children. He wanted to share what he called his "wonders of God" with people who might pay money to hear them. The Mozarts took six-year-old Wolfgang and his sister in the important city of Vienna, Austria. In Vienna, Wolfie promised marriage to the young princess as shared at the opening of this chapter!

Vienna, like other growing cities in Europe in the 1760s, was a center of wealth and culture. Because of better farming and trade, people didn't have to work all the time to survive, so they had extra time to enjoy music and the arts. But this was also before music was recorded, and waaay before music was on tablets and phones! So to hear the latest songs, crowds packed into concert halls. And the richest families actually hired musicians and composers to make music for them every day, like a human radio.

In this popular new world of European music, Wolfgang was a kind of child star. He played for powerful people in important cities, Paris, London, Brussels and Amsterdam. Young Mozart thrilled listeners by doing things no one expected from such a young boy, such as playing blindfolded. He charmed his audiences, once jumping onto an empress's lap and kissing her.

When the Mozarts were not performing, Wolfgang composed music, writing his first *symphony* and his first *opera* before he was 12 years old. These were long pieces of music that told a story and used many instruments at once. Imagine a young boy creating such complicated art. Pretty incredible, right?

Young Wolfgang continued to tour and learn different ways to write music. The family returned to Salzburg, their hometown, in 1771, when

Wolfgang was 15. Now his father was very proud of him but had become very involved in his life after all the years of teaching and touring. Leopold expected Wolfgang's music to support the whole family. Loving his dad, Wolfgang wanted to please him. So at this stage, father and son felt it was time to move beyond youthful tricks on tour and to take on a more serious full-time job in music – he was done being a child star.

Wolfgang would go on to live in Paris and Germany before settling down in Vienna with his wife, Constanze Weber, and their two children. His music earned him a lot of money, but he also spent a lot of it. He was always bold and loved living a big life, buying fine clothing, good food, and fancy parties. Mozart's life was grand but tragically brief; he died young without much money at just 35. But in his short life, Mozart composed more than 600 works across a wild mix of forms: quartets, piano music, violin music, religious music, operas and symphonies. An amazing amount of amazing quality.

Fast forward to you today. It's been about 250 years, and incredibly you would still know many of Mozart's pieces. His *Turkish March* and his *Marriage of Figaro* are still used in movies and TV. You'd probably even know his opening of *Symphony No. 25 in G Minor*, which he wrote as a teenager! Perhaps no one has ever had a greater natural gift for music, and perhaps no one has ever shown it so young.

DISCUSSION GUIDE

Review Questions:

    1. What instrument(s) did Mozart learn first?

    2. How did people listen to music in the 1760s?

    3. Was Mozart very rich when he died?

Discussion Questions:

1. Do you think Mozart's incredible skills in music came from talent or from practicing a lot or both?

2. Do you think it was fair of Mozart's father to expect his son to share his money with the family?

Project Idea:

Mozart Music Memory Challenge. Mozart could hear a piece of music just once and remember every note. Try this memory challenge to see how close you can get!

How to play: Look carefully at the line of letters of music notes below for **10 seconds**. Use a watch/clock, or have a friend count – you'll need your brain free to memorize.

Then close the book or cover it with your hand. Try to say the letters out loud — or write them down in order.

Look back, and check your score!

Beginner Level:

C – D – E – D – C – F – B

Advanced Level:

G – A – A – F – G – B – C – E – D

Mozart Level:

C – E – D – F – D – G – F – C – B – A

Mozart Memory Bonus Twist:

Have a friend read you one of the patterns out loud 2-4 times times instead. Can you repeat it back from memory? Is that easier or harder?

CHAPTER 2

BRAZIL: DOM PEDRO II (1825-1891)

THE KID WHO UNITED AN EMPIRE

Was this boy ready to be emperor? He was only 14! But it didn't matter, they said — they needed him. The empire of Brazil was about to fall apart. Only this teenager, Pedro, could unite the people and save Brazil. In 1840, this boy took the throne and over time did just that — he saved the empire, ruling for nearly 50 years. He earned a special place in history as shown by his nickname, the Magnanimous, which meant he was generous and kind. But all that started when he was just a kid. How did that happen, and what did he do as emperor? Let's read on to learn about Dom Pedro II, the last emperor of Brazil.

Pedro de Alcantara (Pedro II) was born in 1825, the seventh child of Brazil's emperor and the only surviving son. Pedro's mother died just a year after he was born. His father, the emperor, was pushed off the Brazilian throne and went to live in Portugal when Pedro was just five years old. That made Pedro the new emperor, but adults still ran the country because Pedro was so young. In fact, Pedro was so small that he stood on a chair so the crowd could see him when he was introduced to the public as the new emperor. The truth is he was really scared.

Now all that might sound a little strange. If the dad was so unpopular, and folks wanted him to give up his throne, why would they be o.k. with his son as the next emperor? Right? Well the powerful people in Rio de Janeiro, Brazil's capital, were o.k. with Pedro because they thought that they could control him while he grew up. And in many ways that was true. Pedro's advisors had the power until Pedro was old enough. So, as he waited to take charge, he had no mom or dad around. Historians agree that he was sad and lonely. So he studied. A lot.

During the 1830s, when Pedro was still a boy, trouble was brewing in Brazil. Two main groups fought for power while the empire waited for Pedro to be old enough to rule. The two sides were *conservatives* and *liberals*. When conservatives had power, liberals would protest, sometimes violently. When liberals had power, conservatives would try to steal control where they could, like with police. It was like a seesaw — each group was up and down, opposite of the other.

By 1840, Pedro's advisors had lost control. Violent revolts were common. Liberals wanted a change, any change, in leadership. Conservatives wanted a strong voice to bring back order. Pedro was the only answer for everyone, even though he was only 14. So, while they were supposed to wait until he was 18, they crowned him anyway in 1841. And actually, he was ready.

As a teenage emperor in the 1840s, Pedro showed how much he had learned studying and by seeing all the fighting. He wanted to stop conflicts before they happened. He wanted to listen and find solutions. He took charge. He picked strong advisors to put down revolts. Pedro showed he would not put up with the seesaw ride any more.

But Pedro was also curious and approachable. As a teenager he fell in love with photography and got an early camera, one of the very first in Brazil. He had a photo studio made at the palace. The country started to realize that it had a new, young emperor who was going to make a new, modern nation. Indeed, Pedro had the empire back on track before he even turned 20.

So why was he called Pedro the Magnanimous? Let's look at three things that come from his humble nature. First, he listened, letting ordinary people, rich and poor, come to court to share their concerns. Next, he made changes step by step so they lasted. For example, he began a process to abolish (get rid of) slavery by ending the slave trade and then freeing anyone newly born into slavery. Full abolition of slavery came later. You could argue that abolishing slavery *slowly* was wrong, but doing it faster risked civil war and a longer attachment to slavery. Third, he put Brazil ahead of himself. He wore simple clothes in a time when kings and queens wore showy costumes. And when his empire won a war with Paraguay, he preferred sending money to schools over building monuments to the war.

After nearly 50 years as emperor, too many powerful groups, including army leaders, wanted a new system where people would choose the next leader. Older and tired, Pedro didn't fight to stay. He quietly left for Europe. But he had already done so much to change Brazil and its place on the world stage, building railroads and telegraphs and visiting powerful heads of state on other continents. Often in history we see kids who did what their parents did, even if it hadn't worked. Not Pedro. While growing up apart from his dad, the adults around him tried to steer him away from his father's mistakes. It paid off. Dom Pedro II shows us that the best leaders seek to serve those they lead and that kids can turn their families' messes into valuable lessons.

DISCUSSION GUIDE

Review Questions:

1. Why were powerful Brazilians comfortable with Pedro II as a solution when his father left?

2. Later, why did they turn to him to take the crown sooner than planned?

3. Why is Pedro II called Magnanimous?

Discussion Questions:

1. How do you think growing up without his parents changed Pedro II?

2. Do you think Pedro II deserves to be called Magnanimous?

Project Idea:

Photo Essay. Dom Pedro II collected thousands of pictures, capturing all things Brazil from everyday life to modernization projects such as bridges and buildings. His pride in his people and country come through. To understand better his love for home and community, make a photo essay of where you live. Capture the surroundings, both natural and manmade, such as your house, yard, trees, animals, street and car. Snap pictures of the places you visit often: your school, grocery store, parks and playgrounds. Next capture some people in their everyday dress – take pictures of friends and neighbors (with permission!) going about their days or posing on special occasions.

Print the photos and cut them out, gluing them to construction paper that you bind with string or into a notebook. Write captions and dates for the photos. You'll be surprised at how much this essay tells you about *your place*, particularly when you look at it years later. Happy photo hunting!

CHAPTER 3

BRAZIL: PELÉ (1940-2022)

THE TEEN WHO CHANGED SOCCER

The Brazilian national soccer team had a psychologist. That's a doctor who helped with their mental health. This team psychologist would talk to players to make sure they felt ready to play. After he met with 17-year-old Pelé, he said No way — Pelé can't play; he's too young, doesn't have a fighting spirit and doesn't feel a commitment to the team. The coach heard the doctor, but he played Pelé anyway. And wow was that the right call. Because young Pelé went out on the field and made history. Let's read about how.

Pelé was born into a football (Americans call the game *soccer*) home. His full name was Edson Arantes do Nascimento. His father played soccer for a living, but didn't earn much, so the family was proud but poor. Pelé's dad always told how he scored five goals with his head in one game. Pelé's mother was firm and taught her children respect. Once, when Pelé was little, he told his mom that their neighbor had given him a mango. But he had taken the fruit without asking, and his mother caught him in the lie. Pelé never forgot the shame he felt.

Their small front yard of dirt and rocks was their soccer field. Their ball was an old sock filled with newspapers. They played barefoot. But they played all the time, and his dad made Pelé learn skills that would make him great later: the use of both feet, the perfect pass, not just scoring goals. So why was he called Pelé if his name was Edson? Because of soccer, of course. He told his friends at school about a save made by Bilé, the goalie on his dad's team. But he said it wrong, "Pelé" instead of "Bilé." His friends made fun of him for getting it wrong and called him Pelé to tease him. It stuck for the rest of his life.

Pelé's path to soccer stardom was fast. He started playing with local teams, a lot like the youth soccer teams in towns all over the world today. At 13 in 1953, he tried out with 100 other boys to play on the junior version of his father's team, which was coached by a former famous player. That's when things started to get serious. Pelé's coach understood his potential and knew people at Santos FC, a top-level professional club in Brazil. Santos had room for young talent. Pelé's coach told the president of Santos to give Pelé a chance because Pelé could be "the greatest football player in the world." Santos offered him a spot, and Pelé became a professional soccer player at just 15 years old.

He quickly showed he wasn't just another player. He was a complete player with speed, scoring skills, creative moves and vision to make the right pass or guess his opponent's move. He was also beautiful to watch and showed pure joy on the pitch. At 16 in 1957, he was invited to play with the Brazilian national team, and he scored a goal against Argentina. The following year, Sweden was hosting the World Cup, soccer's global tournament of national teams, the game's biggest stage. This is when the team psychologist told the coach not to play Pelé. Then here's what happened in Sweden.

Pelé sat out Brazil's first two games with a hurt knee. In the third game, he finally played. It was against the Soviet Union, and Brazil won, but he felt he should have played better. He thought he would have scored if he "had been more relaxed." Maybe the psychologist was right? Maybe he wasn't ready? Or... maybe he was...

In his second game, this time against Wales, the score was tied 0-0 when Pelé got a pass off his chest with his back to the goal. Popping the ball up once, he wheeled around lightning-fast and "squeezed" a shot into the lower left corner of the goal. Rejoicing, he chased the ball into the net, scooped it up and kissed it! An unbelievable moment. And an unbreakable record? To this day, with that goal, Pelé holds the record for the youngest player to score in the men's World Cup. He was 17 years and 239 days young. "The goal was perhaps the most unforgettable of my career," Pelé later remembered.

Young Pelé wasn't done in Sweden. The next game was the semi-final versus France. Pelé wowed the crowd by scoring three goals, known as a *hat trick*, as Brazil knocked out the French. In the Cup final against the Swedes, the hometown team scored first, but Brazil netted two goals to carry a lead into halftime. In the second half, Pelé took over, scoring two goals to lead Brazil to a 5-2 win. As the referee signaled the end of the game, Pelé fell to the ground and fainted. He was overcome with emotion. He thought of everyone back in Brazil. He remembered how his father had cried when Brazil lost the World Cup in 1950. Now a world champion in 1958, Pelé broke down and cried, halfway around the globe.

Pelé became an international superstar overnight and perhaps the biggest name in international sports that the world had ever known. He would go on to lead Brazil to two more World Cups. He played for and toured the world with Santos for almost two decades. Everyone wanted to see his creative, joyful style. Pelé's enthusiasm was contagious (catchy). In the African nation of Nigeria, for example, the two sides in a civil war agreed to stop the war for 48 hours because Pelé was playing in the country. After retiring from soccer in Brazil, he played for two years in the mid-1970s in New York City, where he helped soccer grow like crazy in the U.S. That was the sheer power of his appeal.

Pelé died in 2022. His amazing story shows that devoting yourself to something you love can be rewarding no matter how old you are. He made sports history before he even turned 18. But no matter how big a hero he became, part of him always remained the modest boy from a simple football house in Brazil. Indeed, when asked later who was the best soccer player who ever lived, he simply said, "The only way to win is as a team."

DISCUSSION GUIDE

Review Questions:

    1. What was the name of Pelé's professional team in Brazil?

2. What record did he set at the 1958 World Cup?

Discussion Questions:

1. Do you think Pelé's coach, who recommended him to the professional team, said that lots of players had the potential to be the best in the world?

2. Why do you think the psychologist thought Pelé wasn't ready? Is it possible that being young and not as committed could make you actually play better?

Project Idea:

Play a young Pelé-style game. Make a soccer ball out of a short sock stuffed tight with newspaper. Once the end of the sock is round-ish, twist the open end and fold the loose sock back over the balled end. If that's just too weird, grab a tennis ball. Next, find a grassy yard. Make two goals on either end of the yard using rocks or sticks or anything you can find as posts. Now remove your shoes. Play one-on-one or two-on-two if you can. The truth is that the barefoot touch of a smaller, less cooperative newspaper (or tennis) ball can actually help your soccer footwork and control when you play with a big, *easy* ball later!

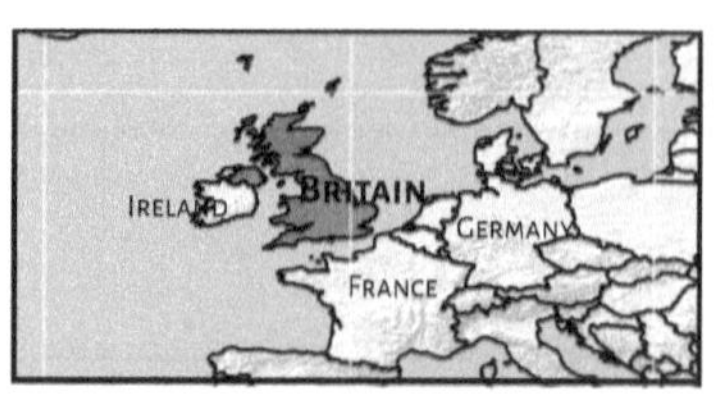

CHAPTER 4

BRITAIN (U.K.): KING EDWARD VI (1537-1553) AND LADY JANE GREY (1537-1554)

KID COUSINS CROWNED IN ENGLAND

Edward VI, the 15-year-old king of England, was very sick, and doctors said he was going to die. He didn't have a child yet or even a wife. So who would be the next king? His top advisors were telling him that he should make his cousin, Jane, the queen. But what about his sister, Mary, who had the natural right to the throne? What would the young king do? What would happen to Jane and Mary? Let's hear more about these young rulers of the 1500s.

His father's "precious jewel," Edward VI was the only son of King Henry VIII. Edward's mom was the third of Henry's six wives! Henry's many wives are actually more than just a historical fun fact — it's the reason that England's rulers changed their religion and stopped being Roman Catholic. You see, Henry wanted a divorce, and that wasn't allowed in the Catholic Church. So Henry said, fine, I'll start my own church so I can get a divorce.

Why did it matter if Henry started a new church? Because some English people followed Henry and left the Catholic church. They were called *Protestants*. But others stayed Catholic. This break-up divided towns and villages and even families. In fact, this split happened right in Henry's own family! His son, little Edward, became a very religious Protestant. But Edward's older sister, Mary, remained Catholic — this will be important later.

After his father, Henry, died in 1547, young Edward became king at just 9 years old. Historians disagree on how much Edward did on his own as king, versus how much was done for him by his advisors, but it was clear that Edward's training and education made him fit to be king. He had the skills for the job. Edward made many changes to religion in England. He replaced Latin language with English during church services. Some religious statues and paintings were removed — in general, Edward supported simpler worship with fewer planned ceremonies.

So when Edward became very ill in early 1553, it made sense for him to pick his *religious Protestant* cousin, Jane, as the next queen (the *heir* to his throne). Plus, Jane was married to Guildford Dudley, whose dad was Edward's closest advisor. See how that works? That's no coincidence. Edward's top helper was Jane's father-in-law, so Edward picked Jane to be the next queen. But it wasn't that easy — Edward's sister, Mary, wanted to be queen too. As a sister, she had the stronger claim and, as a Catholic, had England's Catholics on her side. Who would get the throne?

Let's turn back to cousin Jane. Jane Grey was Edward's and Mary's cousin, technically the granddaughter of Edward's father's sister. Jane was bright and educated and, as mentioned above, very serious about her religion. In truth, her parents had wanted her to marry Edward, but when he got sick, they went after the next best husband for Jane, the son of Edward's closest aide. For her part, Jane had more interest in books than thrones — she dropped to the floor and cried when she found out she was to become queen!

Still, Jane took her royal duties seriously after Edward died on July 6, 1553. On July 10, Jane moved into the English castle, the Tower of London, and became queen at just 15. At the same time, her cousin, Mary, 37, gathered supporters east of the capital to make her own claim to the throne. Mary sent word to Jane that she would not accept Jane as queen and would have the crown for herself! Jane did what she could to stop Mary's claims, but it became clear quickly that Mary had the upper hand. Indeed, with little actual fighting, Mary took the throne, and Jane and her husband were made prisoners in the Tower of London. Jane was queen for just nine days.

Mary wanted to show mercy to her imprisoned cousin, Jane. However, Jane still had some support from powerful people. Even though Jane didn't seem to want the crown personally, just her existence was a threat to Mary. In 1554, Mary made a hard choice.

On a cold February morning, Jane was led to her execution in front of a small crowd in the Tower yard. She stayed strong in the face of death, forgiving the executioner and asking the audience to pray for her. She was then blindfolded, and her hands fumbled for the right spot as she kneeled. She asked, "Where is it?" as a guard helped her. Jane then said a prayer before she was killed. She was just 16 years old.

In turn, Mary's reign would be somewhat short, just 5 years, and she became known as Bloody Mary, but that's another story.

Today, Edward VI is remembered as a son of a king who cared too much about having a son, but also as a talented young monarch who never got a chance. Jane has been widely celebrated as a tragic figure, a pawn (playing piece) in the game of royal chess. Her parents and her husband's family in many ways used her in a very risky play for power

— risky because everyone knew Mary was a strong rival. In the end, the strategy cost a teenage girl her life.

There are a lot of lessons and inspiration to draw from these stories. First, Edward and Jane help us understand that the lives of kings and queens were often far from fairy tales. Edward's wealth could not save him from illness. And Jane's death at the order of her own cousin is horrible, not happily ever after. Next, everyone wants what's best for their children and families, but Jane got pulled into the plans of powerful adults to fulfill their goals, not hers, with results that may give parents caution. Finally, Jane's bravery and sense of duty are inspiring. It's hard to imagine what she went through, but it might help to think of her courage the next time you face a challenge.

DISCUSSION GUIDE

Review Questions:

1. What changes did Edward VI make to religion in England?

2. Why didn't Jane marry Edward?

Discussion Questions:

1. Do you think Edward should have made Mary queen instead of Jane? Do you think he had any choice?

2. Do you think it was fair of the adults to use Jane for their own power? How do you think she felt about it? How would you feel?

Project Idea:

Create your family tree. On a large poster, draw an actual tree with a blank space in the middle. Next, research back as far as you like, but go at least to your grandparents. Then write the names of your grandparents (or as far back as you went) at the top of the tree with connecting lines down the page to your parents and their siblings. Then connecting lines down to you and your siblings and cousins. You can add information like the dates and locations of births. Maybe include pictures? Maybe include pets? If you don't want to do your own family, you could also research the English royal Tudors, which is the family of Edward VI that we just learned about. Either way, this is a great way to think about how important these bloodlines were to royal families.

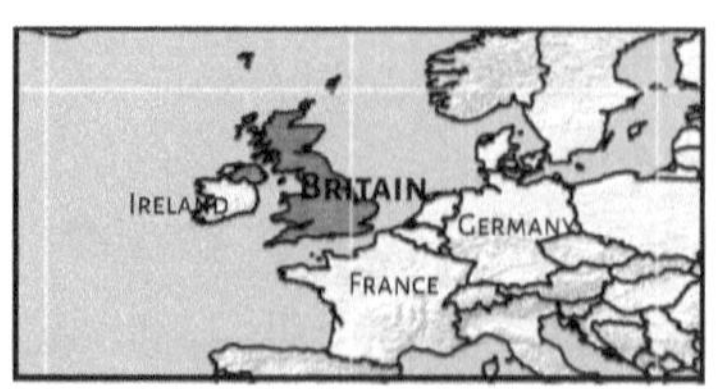

CHAPTER 5

BRITAIN (U.K.): MARY SHELLEY (1797-1851)

TRAILBLAZING YOUNG STORYTELLER

She had to come up with a story. Her friends had challenged her to a ghost-story contest, and she couldn't stop thinking about it. Then one night, she couldn't sleep, and the haunting tale took over her mind. "I have found it!" she wrote, "What terrified me will terrify others." And just like that, a teenager had created a monster that no one would ever forget, even now, more than 200 years later. This is the story of Mary Shelley and her book, Frankenstein.

In June 1816, when she was 18, Mary and her boyfriend, Percy Shelley, went to spend the summer on Lake Geneva in Switzerland. Percy was a writer and poet, and they went with friends, including a famous poet, Lord Byron. They had probably looked forward to boating and hiking and other outdoor summer fun, but a volcano, Mount Tambora, had erupted the year before in Indonesia. Why did that matter halfway around the world in Switzerland? Because the colossal (huge) eruption sent so much ash into the sky that the next year, 1816, was "the year without summer," with darker, colder days and more rain from a volcanic haze. Mary and her friends were stuck inside a lot, and it was gray and gloomy. So they read ghost stories! That led to a ghost-story contest.

Mary's ghost story was the tale of a young scientist, Victor Frankenstein, who used electricity to zap life back into a corpse (dead body). Mary wrote in *Frankenstein*: "By the glimmer of the half-extinguished light, I saw the dull yellow eye of the creature open." Very creepy stuff — and boldly original, especially from a teenager.

Mary's talent, however, did not guarantee success. It was hard for women in her day to get a book published or to compete or even participate in most professions. But Mary's situation was different. Born in 1797 to parents who pushed for reform (change), her mother, Mary Wollstonecraft, had already published a book about the need for girls to get a formal education. Mary's mom sadly died shortly after Mary was born. However, her father, William Godwin, made sure that she was educated. A philosopher (someone who thinks, discusses and writes about life's meaning and how to live), Mary's dad often had people at their home discussing big ideas, such as the creation of humans. It's probably not an accident that Mary's *Frankenstein* involved a man *creating* life and dealing with what came next.

Percy, who became her husband in December 1816, also encouraged Mary to be an author. He was already known in writer's circles, and he actually wrote the introduction to *Frankenstein*. Published in London in 1818 when she was 20 years old, the book did not list Mary — or anyone — as the author. In fact, some people thought *Percy* was the author! To this day, many authors still use pen names, or pseudonyms, sometimes to hide their gender. But even without a named author, *Frankenstein* was a hit. And when it was republished in 1823, Mary's name was on it!

Despite the success of her book, Mary's life in many ways kept the clouds she had over her during the summer of 1816. Her marriage to Percy was stormy, and three of their four children died as infants or in early childhood. Percy himself died tragically in a sailing accident in 1822. Mary was left a widow at 25 with her youngest son, Percy Florence. She never remarried, but continued to write, including additional novels, travel books and reviews. She supported herself well at times, though no work sparked the public's imagination the way *Frankenstein* did.

But Mary had already made history, paving the way for other female authors, and more so, showing that women could write in any genre (type of book). That is, Shelley's *Frankenstein* was not just important as a breakthrough work by a female. It was also an early trailblazer in science fiction — stories based on imaginary new technology, such as travel through time or deep space. Victor Frankenstein gave life through a technological advance, blending new knowledge about electricity with old ideas about reanimation (coming back to life). *Big Hero* 6 and movies like it really come from this tradition.

Today, every kid reading this book is familiar with Frankenstein, which is often used as the name of the monster, though in the book it's actually the scientist. During the Halloween season in America, you'll see versions of the Frankenstein creature everywhere, from scary costumes to candy wrappers to breakfast cereal. Mary's monster is right up there with ghosts, vampires, witches and werewolves! And it all came from the genius of a teenage girl, dreamt up on a stormy night more than 200 years ago.

DISCUSSION GUIDE

Review Questions:

1. Why was it dark and gloomy during the summer of 1816 in Switzerland?

2. Why was Mary's family situation more likely to allow her to be an author?

Discussion Questions:

1. What kind of book would you write if you were writing a book today (history is fun, just FYI)?

2. If you wrote a book, would you want to use your name, a fake name, or no name as the author? Why or why not?

Project Idea:

Write a ghost story. Here are some suggested steps (recalling that I'm a history writer, not a ghost-story writer!).

1. Start with a scary setting, like gloomy woods on a moonless night.

2. Add characters to the setting that are maybe vulnerable, perhaps someone lost or in a hurry.

3. Introduce your ghost - think about something that would scare you.

4. Create a showdown or encounter between the ghost and the other characters.

5. Have the story end with an open question about whether the ghost is real. Or maybe end with a friendly twist as you uncover the real (friendly) source of the ghost. Maybe have your characters

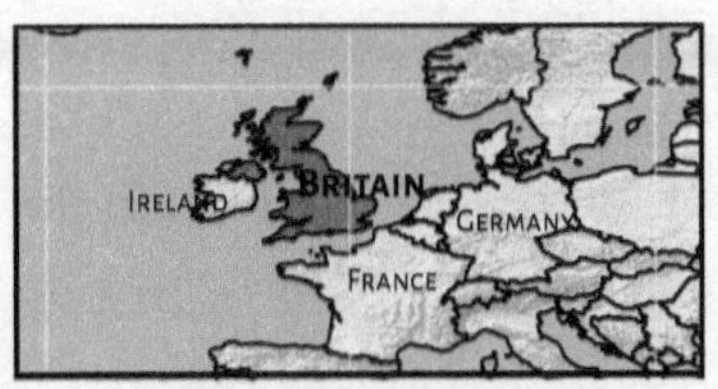

CHAPTER 6

BRITAIN (U.K.): MARY ANNING (1799-1847)

DIGGING FOR DINOSAURS

Mary Anning was ten years old. Her father had died recently, and her family was very poor. Lonely, she went for a walk by herself to the nearby seashore and looked for fossils in the cliffs, the way she used to with her dad. She found a fossil that day and was walking back to her house when a woman on the street saw the fossil in Mary's hand and offered her money for it. Mary was just a young girl but saw right then how she could pitch in for her family! She could help earn a living by hunting for fossils. What she couldn't see then was that her decision to look for fossils would make history. Let's learn how.

Mary Anning might never have grown old enough to make history if it weren't for some luck she had early on. When Mary was a little more than a year old in the summer of 1800, a family friend, Elizabeth, brought her to a horse-riding show in a local field. Taking cover under a large elm tree during a thunderstorm at the show, Mary, Elizabeth and two other women were struck by lightning that hit the tree. The three grown women died, and tiny Mary seemed to be dead too, but she was rushed to a warm bath and survived. It was said that she was a dull baby before the lightning strike, but a bright and lively child after. Whether or not the lighting changed Mary's personality, it was incredible that she lived. She would use the same kind of good fortune for a lifetime of finding fossils.

Lyme Regis, England, where Mary lived all her life, is home to cliffs along the southern coast of the island of Britain. These cliffs are filled with rocks from the Jurassic period, about 201 to 145 million years ago, when dinosaurs walked the Earth and large reptiles swam in the ocean. Whenever the rain and wind peel back layers of rock from the cliffs, new rock is exposed, including Jurassic fossils — plants and animals from long ago preserved in rock. One of the most common is the ammonite, an extinct (no longer living) squid-like creature with a shell that looks like a spiral ram's horn. The round, spiral fossils are really cool looking and can be as wide as a dinner plate. Mary's father, a cabinet-maker, liked to go looking for ammonites in the cliffs and would bring along Mary and her older brother, Joseph.

Formal education was limited for girls during Mary's childhood in England. Still, she grew up in a religious home and learned to read the Bible at church. After her father died in 1810, Mary became determined to help her family by finding and selling fossils, as shared at the beginning of this chapter.

When Mary was about 12, her brother found the skull of an ancient animal in the cliffs and showed it to her. It had big teeth — this was no ammonite! Through winter storms, Mary went looking for the rest of this skeleton. She ran to the beach to see if she could find it whenever it rained. But searching through the layers of rocks was actually dangerous work. The cliffs were not stable — sometimes the rocks would slide beneath your feet, and sometimes the stones above could fall on you. In fact, Mary's beloved dog, Tray, was later killed by rocks that just missed Mary.

Finally, months after her brother had found the skull, little Mary discovered the rest of the creature. It was a 17-foot-long monster! A man paid the Annings 23 pounds for the fossilized skeleton, a lot of money at the time. Still, no one knew what it was. When scientists saw it in London, they thought it was a crocodile. But further study showed it was something else. Scientists named it **ichthyosaur** (ick-THEE-uh-SOAR). Other people had found parts of these animals in the past, but not one so complete. To this day, 12-year-old Mary Anning gets the credit for uncovering the ichthyosaur. Can you picture yourself finding a dinosaur skeleton? Pretty impressive for a kid!

Mary and her family continued to look for and sell fossils in Lyme Regis. At 24, Mary discovered the **plesiosaurus,** a sea reptile that kind of looks like the Loch Ness Monster. This was a major find. At 29, she unearthed a **dimorphodon** skeleton — a flying reptile, the first found outside of Germany. She also helped the world unlock the scientific treasure of **coprolites**; that's fossilized poop! Yup.

For all of these reasons, Mary Anning was later called the "princess of paleontology." Paleontology, the study of fossils, was just starting in the 1800s. People were beginning to understand the age of the Earth. This idea that some animals had lived in the past but vanished — become extinct — was new.

Unfortunately, as a woman in male-dominated circles, Mary did not get much credit during her life for her huge contributions to these new studies. Often, the men who bought her fossils wrote papers about them and got the fame. But over time, Mary's awesome discoveries have come into the light — it's just impossible not to be impressed by what she was able to do on her own, without formal training, education or money — especially as a kid!

Mary has more recently become a powerful symbol of females in science and independent thinking more generally. In 2010, the Royal Society (Britain's oldest club for great scientists) listed her among the "ten most influential British women in science," 163 years after she died. A statue of Mary was unveiled in 2022 in Lyme Regis. It shows her with a hammer in one hand and a fossil in the other at age 23. But *we* know she had already made history when she was only 12.

DISCUSSION GUIDE

Review Questions:

    1. Describe a way that Mary was lucky and a way that she was

not.

2. Name one of the prehistoric creatures that Mary found.

Discussion Questions:

1. Do you think it was fair for the men who paid for Mary's fossils to get the credit for finding them?

2. Mary was very religious and also very interested in science. How do you think those things worked together for her?

3. Why do you think Mary's story has become so popular so long after she lived? What's so special about her life?

Project Idea:

Go on a fossil hunt. You might be surprised to learn that there are many places where you can still find small fossils today. In the U.S., for example, here are some starting places*:

- Around Lake Michigan and Lake Huron, on beaches, you can find *Petoskey Stones*, which are small fossils of coral;

- On ocean beaches on the East Coast, you can find fossilized shark's teeth, particularly where there are a lot of shells. Classic spots include Florida and South Carolina; and

- Public fossil parks and quarry piles where collecting is encouraged, such as Penn Dixie Fossil Park in New York and Mineral Wells Fossil Park in Texas.

*Be sure to check with local collection rules, as the numbers you can take are often limited.

If you're inspired by Mary Anning and can't find a place to hunt for fossils near you, then I would suggest either traveling to a nearby museum with prehistoric bones or models or making an effort to do so on your next family trip. I get that "go to a museum" is not a super-original idea, BUT trust me, there are lots of lesser-known museums out there with fossils and local finds. Universities often have accessible collections too. I bet you'll be surprised by some paleontology that's closer than you think. Happy hunting!

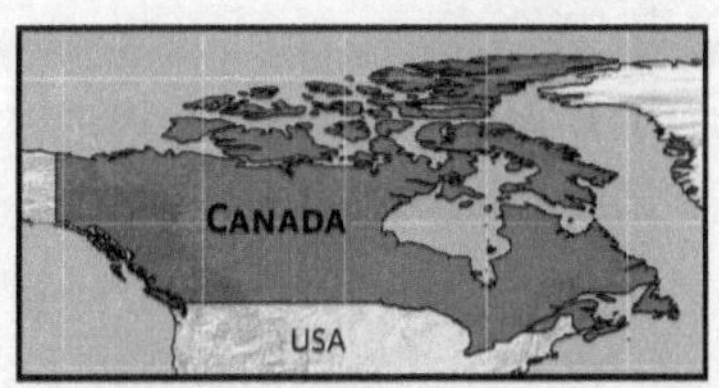

CHAPTER 7

CANADA: MADELEINE DE VERCHERES (1678-1747)

HOLDING DOWN THE FORT AT FOURTEEN

Madeleine knew what was happening because she'd seen this before when she was 12 — an Iroquois war party had come from out of nowhere to surprise them and attack their home. But this time there were no other adults around to lead the defense. This time, at just 14, Madeleine had to take charge... She was outside the fort when the Iroquois attacked, and she started to run back inside when an enemy grabbed the handkerchief she had tied around her neck! What would happen next? Let's hear more about the brave and clever young Madeleine de Vercheres.

Madeleine's father, Francois, had come to New France (now Canada) in 1665 as a soldier in the French Army. They were there to help secure France's North American colony. Together with their Native American allies, the Algonquin and Huron tribes, the French fought against the Iroquois tribe.

When the fighting ended for a time in 1667, Francois decided to stay in New France. For his service to the French king, he received land called Vercheres (rhymes with "fair SHARE"), named for Francois' hometown back in France. He married Marie Perrot, and they had 12 children. Madeleine was number four.

But the fighting never really ended. Living in New France meant a great chance to build a life of fur-trading, fishing, hunting and farming. But it also meant being ready to defend yourself, especially if you lived far from other French settlers like Madeleine's family did. In fact, as the Vercheres village grew, Madeleine's family and the other settlers built a small wooden fort for defense around the manor (main) house, which belonged to her parents. The fort was simple, a rectangle of pointed wooden posts — a *stockade* — a few feet taller than a basketball hoop. Inside the fort, at each corner, was a platform where you could climb to fire your musket. They also had a cannon.

In 1690, the fort was tested. The Iroquois attacked Vercheres unexpectedly when Francois was away. As the landlords, Madeleine's parents were in charge. Her mom, Marie, took command inside the fort as the Iroquois tried to climb the posts to get in. She fired down at the attackers and kept them out until they retreated two days later. Marie was quite an example for her kids! And it mattered...

Because on a chilly fall morning two years later, the Iroquois attacked again. Madeleine and most of the other settlers were busy outside the fort. She was in the garden, and many others were working the nearby fields when the war party snuck out of the bushes and attacked. If the Iroquois caught them, they would be kidnapped or worse. If the raiders got into the fort, their most valuable supplies — muskets, cannon, ammunition, furs — would be taken. Madeleine's parents were away, and she was the oldest living child in the family at the manor. She was now in charge! As the Iroquois started to capture French settlers outside the stockade, she knew what she had to do to save Vercheres. Young Madeleine, just 14, had an idea, but she had to act fast. Here's what she did.

She ran toward the fort. Before she could get there, an attacker grabbed the handkerchief she'd tied around her neck that morning. Thinking quickly, she untied the handkerchief, leaving the warrior holding a cloth but no prisoner. She dashed into the gate, slamming it behind her. Swiftly, she climbed the wall and fired the cannon. Firing the cannon did two things: first, it was a show of force that scared the Iroquois and delayed their attack. Second, it was a cry for help, telling the nearest French forts that Vercheres was in danger. Then she put on a soldier's hat and fired a musket. She told the two soldiers with her to fire their muskets. They yelled and fired their muskets from different places in the fort, staying just hidden below the stockade so that only their hats could be seen. It was a trick - they made it look like the fort was buzzing with armed soldiers, when in truth there were only two, plus one brave teenager.

Madeleine's brilliant plan worked. The settlers stayed safe in the stockade until the Iroquois left; the raiders had lost the element of surprise and eventually retreated with their captives, who were mostly recovered later. Madeleine's quick thinking saved the settlement.

As for the bigger picture, the French and Iroquois agreed to peace in 1701, less than a decade after the attack on Madeleine's home. France was done with mainland colonies in North America by 1803. But by that time French language and culture were there to stay in Quebec, Canada.

Madeleine became a symbol of Canadian courage long after she died. French Canada, in particular, was hungry for a hero after France lost its land in North America. In 1913, a statue of Madeleine was put up in Vercheres, and a plaque there describes how she "took command and defended the post successfully" at "only 14." Then, to recruit women into service in World Wars I and II in the 1900s, the Canadian military used Madeleine's brave tale for motivation. Legend says that Madeleine never cried. Sounds about right.

You can see why her story remains powerful. It's hard to imagine living a life when you could be pressed into battle any morning while working in a garden, even if you're just a teenager. But Madeleine did it. Her smart strategy also reminds us that sometimes it's as good to be clever as strong.

DISCUSSION GUIDE

Review Questions:

1. What brought Madeleine's father to North America?

2. Which tribes were friendly with the French?

Discussion Questions:

1. Do you think it was smart of Madeleine's parents to leave her in charge at the manor?

2. Madeleine's own letter is probably the best source we have for the story shared here. Are there any parts of it that you don't really believe or feel might be stretching the truth?

Project Idea:

Build a fort (shelter) to understand life in the wilderness of New France. Probably the easiest way to make a satisfying shelter is to build a *lean-to*. In the woods, find two trees about 6-8 feet apart, each with a branch at about the same height around shoulder height. Place a long, strong stick horizontally across from one tree to the other, resting on those branches. Note, if you can't find the ideal trees and branches, you could tie the horizontal beam between two trees.

Next, lean long sticks against the beam at an angle to create a shelter beneath them. Cover as much of the length of the beam as you can. Next, use leafy or pine-covered branches to cover gaps between the leaning sticks. As a bonus, create a dry, soft floor with dry leaves or moss.

Note, you can also make a mini lean-to for a toy or stuffed animal — also pretty satisfying and not as demanding.

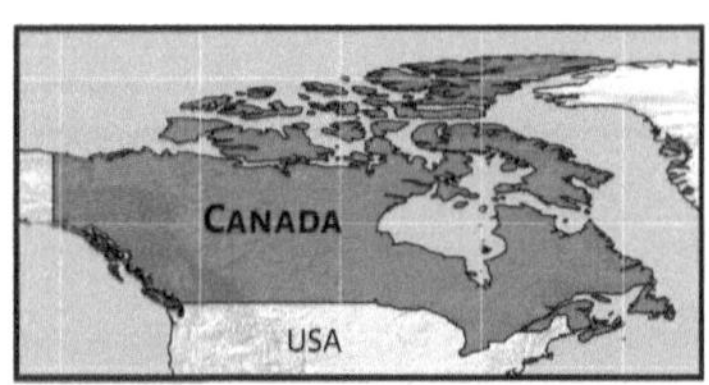

CHAPTER 8

CANADA: JOSEPH-ARMAND BOMBARDIER (1907-1964)

THE INVENTOR WHO WOULDN'T BE SNOWBOUND

The boy dreamed of traveling over the snow-covered roads and trails of the Quebec countryside. He loved engines. He also loved cars. But he didn't love the way cars didn't work in the snow. And before there were plows in the Canadian countryside, you were pretty much stuck in your house or your little village whenever it snowed. And it snowed a lot in this part of Quebec! So Armand spent his life working on ways to travel through snow. This is the remarkable story of how he made history.

Joseph-Armand (Armand) Bombardier was a whiz with machines as a little boy in Valcourt, Quebec, Canada. He was the oldest of eight kids, and his father hoped he would be a Catholic priest. But Armand liked making gadgets that moved and spun and tinkering with motors. At 13 in 1920, using parts from an old clock, he figured out how to make the wheels turn on his little brothers' toy trains. His big dream was to build something that could move over snow, to help people get around in winter in remote villages like his.

As a teenager, Armand took apart his parents' car, just for fun. He did put it back together. But his father was worried he'd do it again, so his dad got him an old Ford car engine to mess around with. This gift might have changed history! Here's how.

At just 15, Armand used that old Ford motor to build his first snow vehicle. Picture a long sled like the old-fashioned kind with metal runners; now add a propeller behind it. It was incredibly loud and dangerous with a large open propeller. You could lose a finger, or worse! So, even though it showed promise, Armand's dad made him take it apart... Have you ever heard one of those stories about rock stars whose parents were always asking them to turn down their electric guitars, never knowing that that guitar would someday make their kid rich and famous? This is a little like that. And just like those young rockers who kept turning up their guitars, Armand kept working on his inventions.

When he was 17, Armand proved to his family that he was serious about engineering, and he went away to Montreal to work and take classes to learn how to be a mechanic. So his father didn't get Armand to become a priest. But his parents did get him to come home, back to the countryside, to start a mechanic's garage in Valcourt. Armand's family helped get him set up, and at 19, he opened his repair business.

Armand's garage was successful, and became known for being able to fix anything. It might have helped that he already had a reputation as the boy who made toys move and built a crazy, loud sled with a propeller! He married Yvonne Labrecque when he was 22, and they had six children. He kept a passion for his work, laboring around the clock. He used any spare time — nights, weekends, holidays — chasing his dream to make a vehicle for travel over snow.

When Armand was 26, tragedy struck him and Yvonne. Sick with an infection in his belly, their two-year-old son could not get to the hospital and potential life-saving medicine because they were trapped in their village by snow. Sadly, their little boy died. It was exactly the problem that had always haunted Armand. Now he worked even harder to invent the solution.

There were a number of challenges for snow vehicles: they had to have enough traction to move through all kinds of snow — powdery snow, icy snow, wet snow, packed snow. And they couldn't be so heavy that they sank. In about 1935, Armand solved these problems with a lightweight motor and tracks made with two rubber bands connected by light steel rods. The tracks ran over wheels with teeth. The teeth would catch between the steel rods to move the tracks. The Bombardier snowmobile was born.

In 1937, Armand started to sell his B7, the *Bombardier 7*, for seven passengers, as the answer for doctors, priests and postal carriers who needed to get to rural places in winter. Transforming his Valcourt garage into a snowmobile-making shop, he hired his siblings and local farmers to make snowmobiles. Just ten years later they had a new factory that could make 1,000 in a year! No one complained about Armand's tinkering anymore — no one told this rock star to turn down his guitar.

After 1948, local governments began to plow roads for cars in winter, and sales of Bombardier's larger snowmobiles slowed. Armand had been determined to make machines that saved people like his son, but he had to adjust. His last great accomplishment was coming up with a new kind of snowmobile. It wasn't so much a solution for unplowed roads, but a vehicle to have fun in the winter where no one else could go. They called it the Ski-Dog at first, but by mistake changed the "g" to an "o," and liked it so much the name stuck: *Ski-Doo!* In 1959, the small, lightweight Ski-Doo was launched for one or two riders, the first snowmobile that could be mass-produced (made in big numbers with the same parts over and over). When Armand died at age 56 in 1964, they were already making more than 8,000 Ski-Doos a year!

Today, BRP (Bombardier Recreational Products) still makes snowmobiles. Armand's dream of a vehicle to access rural winters has become more about riders having fun in the snow. But his invention's story is a remarkable example of someone seeing a problem and working tirelessly to solve it. He found his passion at a young age and went after it, even when people around him tried to make him stop. And his final invention, the Ski-Doo, once again captured the fun and winter spirit of the noisy propeller sled that he built when he was just 15.

DISCUSSION GUIDE

Review Questions:

1. What early examples from his childhood showed Armand's mechanical talent?

2. What kinds of people first needed his large snowmobile? Why?

Discussion Questions:

1. When the Bombardier snowmobile company started to grow, Armand had his family work for him. Would you do the same? Why or why not?

2. Bombardier started to focus on smaller snowmobiles built for fun instead of larger ones built for practical purposes. Can you think of other inventions that started out for one purpose but were eventually used for something else?

Project Idea:

Invent something you need. Think of a problem to solve in your life — too much screen time or not enough vegetables at dinner or something else. Think of two inventions that could solve the problem. Take notes on how the inventions work and draw a picture of each.

Next, think about the process you will go through to make this solution come to life — will you need help? A big factory? Lots of time and money?

Finally, make a list of the strengths and weaknesses of each solution — is one easier to make, easier to use or less likely to need repairs? Present your ideas to an audience, including the strengths and weaknesses, and have them vote on the preferred solution.

You could also do this with a partner and find out whose solution is better! Either way, this project will help you understand the work that Joseph-Armand Bombardier did to create his snowmobiles.

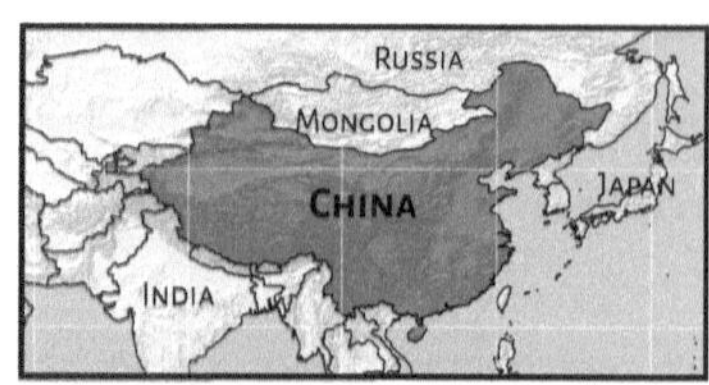

CHAPTER 9

CHINA: PUYI (1906-1967)

THE END OF THE EMPERORS

Peek inside a Chinese public garden in the 1960s. Picture an older man stepping carefully among the plants and flowers, pulling weeds and trimming branches. He lives in a simple room inside the walls of the garden. As he works, this gardener thinks about where he used to live as a boy, where his servants did the gardening. He remembers that he could have had any flower that he wanted when he was a child, any fruit he could think of. That's because this man shuffling to his tiny home is not just any handyman. He is Puyi (pronounced pooh-yee), *and as a kid, he was the emperor of all of China! How did he go from palaces to pruning? Read on to learn his one-of-a-kind story.*

Out of nowhere, the palace guards and helpers suddenly appeared at Puyi's house in Beijing (pronounced *bay-JING*, rhymes with *hey, king!*). The year is 1908. The emperor had just died, and Puyi had been named the new emperor. He was just two years old. There was no warning, no invitation. The guards scooped up the toddler, and he screamed for his mom and dad and tried to kick himself free. They put little Puyi in a fancy covered box on poles that they quickly carried away. Puyi cried;

he was terrified. He didn't understand, but he was right to be scared — he wouldn't see his mother again for seven years.

Crowned emperor two weeks later, Puyi's childhood in the Forbidden City (the huge Chinese royal compound with nearly 1,000 buildings) was far from normal. He later said it was kind of like living in a "yellow mist" because everything — his walls, chairs, pillows, clothes, curtains, cups and bowls — was the special color yellow for the emperor. In that golden world, he was treated like a god. People turned away and knelt down whenever he walked by. His meals were a giant variety of everything you could imagine. People followed him wherever he went in the palace with snacks, a change of clothes and medicine. The whole thing would look silly to anyone today.

But it wasn't silly to many of the hungry citizens of China. Years of wars had created a lot of anger in China, and people were tired of the old ways and the riches of the palace. By 1912, revolutionaries had defeated the royal government and forced Puyi to give up the throne. Emperors had ruled China for more than 2,000 years, but this was finally the end. It all came to a stop when Puyi was just six years old.

The new leaders did not want to change too much too fast. So while Puyi no longer had power as emperor, he was allowed to stay where he lived in the Forbidden City, where only certain people were allowed. For Puyi, not much was different. He hadn't been doing a lot of ruling as a six-year-old — that was for his advisors. So he just kept on being worshipped within the safety of the royal grounds. He continued growing his long, braided hair down his back. He married a beautiful woman he chose from a set of photos when he was 16 in 1922.

But China outside the palace walls was still in conflict and far rougher than Puyi's pampered world. When Puyi was about 18, he was finally forced out of the Forbidden City. He and his wife fled to the northeast as many different groups fought for control of China. There, Puyi eventually teamed up with the Japanese. When he was in his late 20s, Japan took over northeast China and made Puyi ruler of that part of the country, calling him "emperor" once again. But the truth was that he still didn't have any real power. He had fancy clothes and a nice house, but the Japanese made all the important decisions.

After Japan lost World War II in 1945, the Japanese left northeast China. Because he had been a friend to Japan, Puyi tried to escape but was caught and soon became a prisoner in his home country. The Chinese

Communist Party took over China in 1949. Puyi was "re-educated" by the communists in prison. Now in his 40s, he had to learn to tie his shoes and brush his teeth for himself, to understand how his people lived. He got ordinary jobs working for the government: street sweeper, gardener, and office work. He died a quiet death as a common Chinese man in 1967 at 61.

Puyi's life was at an incredible turning point in Chinese history. It's rare that one single person could be part of all these world events. Other powerful people right in this book didn't survive big childhood turning points; Anastasia Romanov and Lady Jane Grey died in situations like Puyi's.

Maybe that's why so many people have chosen to learn about China through Puyi's story — the movie "The Last Emperor" was a huge hit long after his death. Puyi was a historic kid, but over time, history started to happen around him, beyond him, as it does for most people. Think about that. In order to survive, he had to become *normal*. A lot of history tells the opposite tale: regular people who do something remarkable. So Puyi's life stands out in history — he was an *emperor* who became *one of us*.

DISCUSSION GUIDE

Review Questions:

1. What were some of the things that made Puyi's childhood so different from a normal upbringing?

2. What were some of the things Puyi had to learn as an older man that most children do for themselves?

Discussion Questions:

1. Why do you think the emperors in China were treated in such special ways? Do you think that kind of treatment made for better or worse leaders? Why?

2. Puyi wrote his own biography after his "re-education" by the Communist Party. Do you think he was completely truthful in his autobiography? Why or why not?

Project Idea:

Write your autobiography. Puyi wrote an autobiography he called *From Emperor to Citizen*, which told about his life, including his childhood on the throne. To tell your story, first outline the big events:

- Where you were born

- Your family, any siblings or pets

- Your homes (any moves?)

- Your schools

- Big trips

- Your favorite things to do, when you started doing them and how they've changed for you

- What you hope for in the future

Fill in the gaps with how you felt in each of these times or what people have told you about them if you can't remember (like when you were born). For example, don't just say "I have a dog." Instead, talk about how it felt when you got your dog, how you named the dog, what it's like to have the dog now, what you do with the dog. Ask and answer the same questions — how, what, why — for each part of the outline, and you'll have a great story!

CHAPTER 10

COLOMBIA: PEDRO PASCASIO MARTINEZ
(1807-1885)

THE PEASANT BOY WHO REFUSED GOLD

Poor boys like Pedro from the countryside did not go to school. Why would anyone need to learn schoolwork when they were going to sell firewood and work on farms, people thought. Indeed, when Pedro was old enough, still a little boy, he had to help earn money. He found work as a stable boy and servant for the Leivas, an important family in town. Who would have guessed that Pedro's job at the Leivas would lead to a life-and-death meeting between Pedro and a powerful enemy soldier? And a decision that would change history.

As a boy, Pedro Pascasio Martinez was skinny and not very tall and wore a wide straw hat. Born into a poor farming family in 1807, Pedro helped his parents earn money by selling firewood. He would help gather wood and then carry it to the town of Belén, barefoot or in sandals, to offer at the Leivas and other nicer homes. Well-off landowners like Juan Leiva lived near the church, which was the center of life in colonial Colombia and where news was exchanged. When he was old enough, Pedro began work as a servant-boy at the Leivas, taking care of their horses and cows and doing chores around the house.

In 1807, the land that is now Colombia was part of a larger colony controlled by Spain. By the time Pedro was working at the Leivas, Juan Leiva was a local leader in a struggle to win Colombian independence from the Spanish. Around the Leiva house, Pedro heard a lot of talk about this goal to free Colombia. It was exciting to think about, both for the wealthy Leivas, who wanted to run things on their own, and for peasants like Pedro, who hoped to get more opportunities from new leaders. Pedro became a patriot, a believer in Colombia's independence.

Juan Leiva hosted many important patriot meetings at his house. When Pedro was 12, a leader of the independence movement, General Simón Bolívar , was taking his army on a daring march over the mountains. They were on their way to try to kick the Spanish army out of the Colombian capital. Bolívar and his soldiers passed through Belén along the way.

While in Belén, Bolivar spent the night at the Leiva's and saw how good a worker Pedro was. Before Bolivar left, he asked Pedro to join the march. Pedro's job would be to take care of Bolivar's horse, Muchacho.

This was big. Suddenly, little, humble Pedro was at the side of the man still honored today as the liberator of Colombia.

Three weeks after Bolívar's army marched away from Belén, they met the Spanish army at Boyacá in a crucial battle. The patriots won a huge victory in just two hours. That night, Pedro took Muchacho to graze near a small river. A young Black soldier, José, went too. As the boys approached some boulders near the water, they saw movement among the rocks in the moonlight...

Now no one knows exactly what happened next, but history tells a number of versions of the story that all have the same key details, which are included here. So, because that day's battle had just ended and ended so quickly, many of the Spanish soldiers weren't able to get away. Some were taken prisoner, but some hid, afraid they would be killed if captured.

Pedro and José knew enemy soldiers were still around. So seeing something move in the boulders, they grabbed their weapons, left the horses and tiptoed toward the stones in the quiet night air. Suddenly, two enemy soldiers came out of hiding! José ran after one and shot him. At the same time, Pedro wounded the other with his spear and then pinned him down with the sharp point. Fearing for his life, Pedro's foe told him that he was Colonel José María Barreiro, the commander of the Spanish soldiers! Colonel Barreiro knew that he was in big trouble, so he played the only card he had. Alone with Pedro, the colonel pulled out a bag of gold and offered it to Pedro to let him go. Pedro was poor, as we know, and this money could have changed his life and his family's. But he was loyal to the other freedom fighters. Proudly, he told the colonel that no amount of gold could buy his country's freedom. He took his prisoner back to camp.

Arriving back at camp, Pedro and José got in trouble at first. *Where had Muchacho been for so long?* But all was quickly forgiven when Bolivar saw that Pedro had captured Colonel Berriero. As a reward, Pedro was given the rank of sergeant and promised to be paid more later. The 11-year-old was a hero.

Capturing Colonel Barreiro turned out to be important for the patriots; Berriero was not able to help the Spanish army regroup, and the huge loss at the Battle of Boyacá basically ended the fighting. Bolivar and his army of patriots took the capital three days later. Over the coming decades, many different groups would lead the government of independent Colombia, but the country would never again be ruled by Spain.

Pedro never really got the full reward he was promised for his bravery. When he was very old, he went to the capital to tell leaders who he was and what he had done. They agreed that he should get payments, but the trip to pick up the money was long and cost more than the payments. Pedro died a poor farmer in 1885, much as he had been born. But his descendants have worked to keep his heroism alive.

And there they have succeeded. Today, monuments in Colombia honor Pedro's integrity (doing the right thing) and give his family a lasting heroic legacy (memory). In his hometown of Belén, a statue of Pedro stands beside a wall that honors great Colombians. At the Boyacá battlefield, a sculpture shows him and José in action among the rocks. And fittingly, the Colombian army's training school is named after Pedro, reminding soldiers that their honesty and loyalty is as important as the fighting skills they learn.

DISCUSSION GUIDE

Review Questions:

1. Why weren't families like Pedro's concerned about formal education?

2. How did Bolivar meet Pedro? What did Pedro do as a helper for Bolivar?

Discussion Questions:

1. Do you think Pedro truly became a believer in the fight for Colombian independence?

2. How do you think the conversation between Pedro and Colonel Barreiro actually went?

3. Do you think Pedro was rewarded fairly for his heroics? Why was he treated the way he was after the war?

Project Idea:

Would You Rather. As you think about Pedro's tough decision, here are some thought-provoking *would-you-rathers*. This will help you and your friends understand the difficult moment Pedro faced.

Would you rather...

- Go to school or work on a farm

- Live in town or live in the country

- Take care of horses or goats

- Milk cows or collect eggs from hens

- Carry firewood or do dishes

- March on a long road or hike up a mountain

- Be an army soldier or a navy sailor

- Be ruled by a king/queen or vote for a president

- Have a plaque made about you or a school named after you

- Read a history book or do *would-you-rathers*

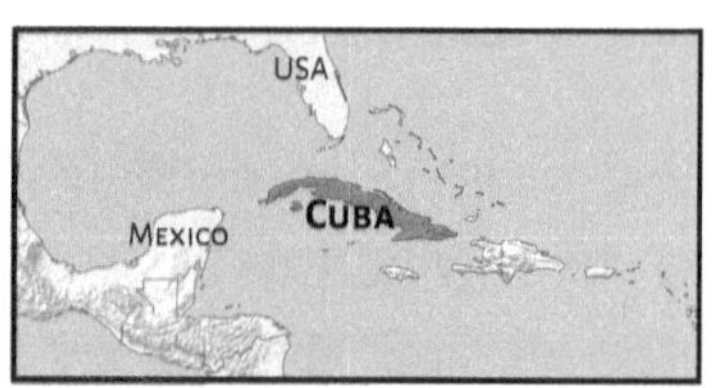

CHAPTER 11

CUBA: JOSÉ MARTÍ (1853-1895)

THE YOUNG VOICE AND SOUL OF OF AN ISLAND

This boy from Cuba had a way with words. He made powerful arguments that sounded like poetry. He captivated people. But when he wrote angry things about Spain, the Spanish sent young José to prison to silence him. Just 16 years old, his punishment was brutal: hard labor mining limestone rocks in a quarry (a huge pit). There, the chains on his ankles cut deeply into his legs, and the quarry dust stung his eyes. The scars lasted a lifetime, but so did José's will to free Cuba from Spain. Let's read about the incredible life of José Martí, the voice and soul of Cuba.

José's family was poor growing up, but they were better off than many and had enough to survive. In 1800s Cuba, just a small group of families were very rich. These were owners of sugar plantations. As a boy exploring the fields of the Cuban countryside, José was horrified at the way African slaves were treated as they worked the sugarcane on those plantations. Some say he saw the cruelty with his own eyes, and he never forgot.

Indeed, José had a passionate heart — he showed promise as an artist, studying drawing as a teen. But he also had a very sharp brain for schoolwork. A teacher took notice and encouraged him to learn with older students. José read about *abolition*, the movement to end slavery, in America. He wished for the same thing in Cuba. He wanted equality for all the different kinds of people who called the island home.

Also, Cuba was surrounded by independent countries that had broken free from vast European empires — Mexico from Spain, Haiti from France and the United States from Britain. But Spain's leaders, across the Atlantic Ocean in Europe, still controlled Cuba and the inequality there. José looked at these other countries and dreamed of an independent Cuba where they would choose their own leaders.

In 1868, Cubans began a revolution to end Spain's rule. A year into this new war, 15-year-old José teamed up with a friend to start their own newspaper to spread support for Cuban independence. José also published a play supporting the Cuban rebels. Young José wrote with both his heart and his brain, the feeling of an artist with the fire of a general. In his play, he promised: "The slave has always shaken off his yoke." This was rebellion as poetry!

Within months, José was arrested for what he wrote, as shared at the start of this chapter. After his legs were injured in the prison quarry, he was removed from the mine and eventually exiled (sent away) to Spain in 1871. Still only a teenager, he had been banished from his own country. His voice already had a big impact when he was just a kid. Think about that for a moment — so many historic heroes are remembered for what they did on the battlefield or in the halls of government. Jose is in this book for what he did with his writing as a teenager. Inspiring stuff for anyone who likes to write — in a diary, as a pen pal, your own stories – your pen can be as mighty as a sword. Now back to the story...

That 1868 Cuban rebellion eventually failed. But for young José, the fight was just the beginning. In Spain, José continued to learn about philosophy (the study of basic truths) and government. He longed to go back to Cuba to share his ideas there about freedom from Spain, but he was not allowed. So José spent time all over, in Mexico, Guatemala, Venezuela, and eventually New York City, supporting the cause of Cuban independence wherever he went. He married and had a son in the 1870s. And he continued to write from both sides of this personality — his artistic and his political. In fact, he ran a magazine for kids at the same time that he was planning the battle for Cuban freedom! José was a fighter with feelings, writing: "*We work for children, because children are those who know how to love, because children are the hope of the world.*" You can see how Jose was a really special blend of talents.

José worked endlessly to free Cuba, speaking and writing from New York and Florida in the 1880s and 1890s. He never stopped. José was somewhat small as an adult but said to be an awesome speaker. He was always well-dressed and impressive on stage. Over time, this natural leader became a voice not only for Cuba but for all of Latin America. José famously urged Latin America to build up its nations without Europe or America: "Our wine should be made from what we have — and even if it turns sour, it's still our wine!" So colorful for political speech!

At 42 in 1895, José finally returned to Cuba with other exiles ready to fight. But tragedy struck quickly. Riding on his horse into an early skirmish, a small battle, José was shot and killed by Spanish soldiers. Sadly he didn't live to see it, but thanks in part to everything he did – and said — his beloved island of Cuba would finally become independent seven years later.

Today, José Martí remains a hero to Cubans for both sides of his unique personality. He is remembered as one of the great Spanish-language writers but also a powerful force for freedom. With such an unusual set of gifts, maybe it's not a surprise that he is embraced by both communists and capitalists from Cuba. The island's largest airport bears his name, as do statues in U.S. But he started his fight for freedom and became an exile only because he wielded a fearless pen as a teenager. Jose's story reminds us that revolutionaries don't always carry rifles. His life also tells us something amazing that applies outside big historical events: your voice might break through the noise and be heard better if you find a new way to say things — your message might stick if it's delivered in an unexpected way.

DISCUSSION GUIDE

Review Questions:

1. What talents did José Martí have? Why was he an effective leader?

2. Provide an example of something he wrote.

Discussion Questions:

1. Why do you think he was punished so harshly for his anti-Spain writing? Do you think that could happen today?

2. José Martí was living in the U.S. when he urged Latin America to avoid American control — what do you think he learned living in America that made him feel that way?

3. Can you think of someone who has been heard better thanks to a different way of sharing his or her message?

Project Idea:

Write a diary entry as if you are José Martí. Pick a time in his life: his teenage years writing about independence, his time in prison, his time studying in Spain, his life in New York or when he finally returned to free Cuba. Consider what he was thinking at the time, what he wanted for Cuba and how that was impacting whatever he was doing every day. Add details about what he's learning at that time and how you might feel. Are you sad? Hopeful? Frustrated? Excited? As a colorful writer, he may have included a couple of verses of poetry in his diary — try to do that as a bonus! This project will help you get into the mindset of someone who was kept away from his home and missed it but kept working to get back.

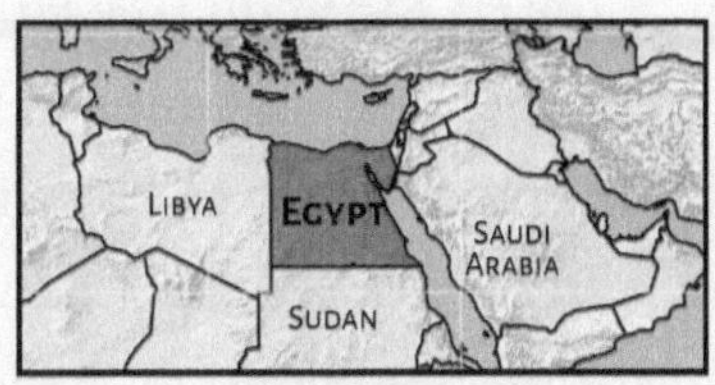

CHAPTER 12

EGYPT: UMM KULTHUM (1904-1975)

THE SINGER WHO STOPPED TRAFFIC

You might have heard that you can't be all things to all people. And that's probably true for most — chasing one goal often means letting go of another. But this idea doesn't apply to the incredible life of Umm Kulthum. This amazing Egyptian singer somehow captured the ears and hearts of everyone, old and young, men and women, rich and poor. Indeed, when she died at 71 in 1975, 4 million people came to her funeral! They climbed rooftops to see her parade and sobbed in the streets. How did Umm manage to be all things to all Egyptians? Perhaps because she never forgot who she was as a kid. Here's her story.

The Egypt of Umm Kulthum's (*pronounced OOM cool-SOOM*) childhood had a lot in common with the Egypt of today. A ribbon of farms and villages lined the huge Nile River. Most people lived in small countryside villages, but the biggest city was the ancient but busy modern capital, Cairo. Most of the population was Muslim, like Umm's family, and Egyptians were proud of their long history, including the famous pyramids.

One important difference in young Umm's Egypt versus today: the British controlled Egypt, at least as far as the big decisions. British soldiers and officials were seen out and about, especially in the cities.

Many Egyptians were angry about the British presence and wanted independence for their country. More on this later.

Umm was born in 1904 in a tiny farming village in the Nile River Delta, near where the river empties into the Mediterranean Sea. Umm's father was the prayer leader in a local mosque, a Muslim place of worship. This role gave Umm's family good standing in their religious rural community, but it did not provide much money. They lived very humbly in a mud-brick house. To earn extra, Umm's dad sang religious songs at celebrations — holidays and weddings. He was also teaching his son, Umm's older brother, how to sing, kind of passing down the family business. At the same time, as the daughter of a prayer reader, Umm was learning to read the Qur'an (*pronounced koo-RAHN*), the Muslim holy book.

Umm revealed how special she was when she was just a little kid. She showed an amazing ability to pronounce and remember the words of the Qur'an. She also learned the songs on her own that her dad was teaching her brother — her father wasn't even trying to teach her! Umm's clear reading and musical gifts amazed her dad. He wanted to bring her with him for his performances — her singing would make him sound so much better!

But there was one big problem; she was a girl. Women in their villages weren't allowed to sing religious songs in public. What was Umm's father going to do? Follow the rules and leave her voice at home? No way. When she was just six or seven, he dressed her up as a boy and brought her along.

But Umm was such a good singer that after a while it didn't matter that she was a girl. Wealthy village leaders around the Nile Delta wanted to hear her. They were awed by the power of her pipes. Once she even got a tip equal to half of her father's mosque salary. Before she was 10, she was a popular local performer and on her way to being the family's star. And she was still just a kid.

By the time she was in her late teens, her family decided to move to Cairo to help her music career. Despite that big bet, Umm was careful about becoming a famous performer. That's because, at the time, many people looked down on singers, especially women from poor families who sang in public, even in the city. So at first she balanced her powerful voice and feminine appearance by singing traditional religious songs and wearing modest, farmer-style clothing.

But that caution didn't stop her rise to fame. Her voice was unforgettable. As she became more popular, she spread her artistic wings. Umm began wearing more modern — but still modest — dresses. When she was in her early 20s, she made a brave change; she hired her own band of Cairo musicians. She blended their international instruments with traditional Arab poetry — poems that told stories true to her rural roots. Mixing modern Cairo with her village soul, Umm recorded 14 records before she turned 22. They sold like crazy because she was popular in the city and in the countryside, like a country-pop crossover queen a century before Taylor Swift.

All that would be enough to make her story worth including in this book. But why did four million people go to her funeral 50 years later? First, beginning in her 30s, she performed a monthly radio concert that the whole country listened to. Traffic would literally stop each month during these radio shows. She also starred in hugely popular movies about romance, loyalty and ordinary Egyptians doing the right thing.

But she was bigger than music and movies. She became president of the Egyptian musicians, a role no woman had ever had. Then in the 1950s, Egypt's new leaders pushed the last British soldiers to leave, and Umm belted out powerful songs supporting full independence. Maybe even larger than any one event, though, she helped create a sense of what it meant to be Egyptian and maybe even what it meant to be Arab in the modern world. That is, for many in the Middle Eastern countryside who couldn't read, she brought them Arabic poetry they would never have heard. These stirring tales of love, loss, history, religion and everyday life came over the radio in her voice. It was the voice of a woman who grew up in a village and understood them. For that, they called her "The Voice of Egypt" and "Egypt's Fourth Pyramid." For that, they climbed rooftops to say goodbye.

DISCUSSION GUIDE

Review Questions:

1. How did Umm's father's jobs as prayer leader and singer impact her music career?

2. What made Umm so much more famous in the 1930s and after?

Discussion Questions:

1. Does every singer represent a place or a culture? Can you think of singers who do more than others?

2. Do you think someone could be as popular today telling stories that come from religious teachings?

Project Idea:

Voice of [place] Music Star Poster. Think of a music artist who represents your home or somewhere else, like Umm is the *Voice of Egypt*. For example, think of Beyoncé for Houston or Bruce Springsteen for New Jersey. Now make a poster advertising their concert or radio show as the "voice of" that place, like "BTS: Voice of South Korea."

Title the poster at the top with the "voice of _______" or something clever like Umm's "The Fourth Pyramid" nickname. Then draw the artist and some items that represent the place, such as a skyline, famous food, sports team, event or small map. Include a date and location for the show and then a line or two at the bottom about the music, for example, "this singer makes people feel _______," or "his/her songs talk about _______." This will help you think about how Umm shaped a national feeling.

CHAPTER 13

ETHIOPIA: JAGAMA KELLO (1920-2017)

LEADING RESISTANCE FROM THE HILLS

Jagama could've stayed at home. His family was well off, and he was well cared for. But when invaders from Italy started marching on Ethiopia, his home country, he felt that he had to act. He had to do something. So at 15, without a weapon, without a plan and without a roof over his head, he left home to fight for his people. This is the remarkable story of how young Jagama Kello became the soldier called Thunderstorm! Let's read more.

For some background for his chapter, when Jagama Kello was a kid in the 1930s, Ethiopia was an independent African nation ruled by Emperor Haile Selassie. Decades before in the 1880s and 1890s, Ethiopia had defeated Italy in a war that most of Europe had expected Italy to win. With newer weapons and training at the time, European forces had captured many parts of Africa in the 1800s. But when Ethiopia beat the Italians, it shocked people. Italy was badly embarrassed.

When Benito Mussolini later became the ruler of Italy in the 1920s, Italy still cared a lot about Ethiopia's land. Why? Because Italy had other colonies in the Horn of East Africa next to Ethiopia. So to unite his colonies and maybe to get some revenge, Mussolini set his sights on

Ethiopia. In 1935, Italy invaded Ethiopia again. All this sets the stage for Jagama Kello's story.

Jagama was born around 1920 in a small town near, Addis Ababa, Ethiopia's largest city. His father was wealthy and owned more than 900 acres of land, which is about twice the size of the usual family corn farm you might see driving through America today. Jagama and his older brother grew up comfortable among their family's fields in the Ethiopian countryside.

In 1935, Jagama was living safely on his parents' farm, just 15 years old. That's when the Italian army invaded. Italy took over two Ethiopian cities in less than two weeks. It became clear that this second war might not go as well for Ethiopia — the Italians had more tanks, more planes, more cannons and more machine guns. The Ethiopians only had horse-drawn carts and were badly outgunned.

Jagama and his brother couldn't just let Italy march through their proud country. They left home and joined the resistance fighters, the *patriots*. They lived in the *bush*, camping under the stars in the wilderness. Jagama did not even have a gun when he started fighting, but in some ways, he didn't need one. The patriots used *guerrilla warfare* — small, fast attacks when the Italians weren't expecting it. They rolled boulders off cliffs onto troops and trucks. They cut telephone lines and stole guns and ammunition. Over time, these patriots gathered better equipment than the actual Ethiopian military. Jagama even got a rifle. Despite this strong resistance from Jagama and the guerrillas, by 1936 the Italians had taken the Ethiopian capital and sent Emperor Selassie on the run to Britain.

But the patriots wouldn't quit. They kept Ethiopian control of many places in the countryside and the mountains. Jagama became a leader among the guerrillas. He grew out his hair into a huge *afro*, which he said scared his enemies. He had no training as a soldier, but he recruited peasants by the hundreds. They followed this teenage warrior on hit-and-run missions, kidnapping Italian messengers and setting fire to Italian camps. Jagama never let up. For five years, he kept fighting — he'd grown up with powerful people and knew how to take charge, using his wealthy upbringing to become a leader of an army when he might have used it to be safe. People started calling him *Thunderstorm* for his courage and determination.

When he was about 20, he led a raid on an Italian fort, routing the Italian soldiers and taking 2,000 rifles. He was able to arm more recruits, and the number of soldiers under his command grew to more than 3,000. Soon after, in 1941, World War II spread to the Horn of Africa. The British and other Allies joined the war on the side of Ethiopia, and they started to beat Italy, even retaking the capital.

With the war getting better for Ethiopia, Emperor Selassie returned from Britain. He invited Jagama to the Ethiopian capital to team up with the British against the Italians, but Jagama refused to go. He wondered, *Why should I trust the British when they weren't fighting for Ethiopia the whole time?* So Emperor Selassie came to Jagama instead! When the emperor arrived at Jagama's camp, Jagama paraded his 3,500 troops for him to show the power of the guerrillas. They had armed themselves, stood up to Italy and survived, led by a teenager! Seeing their strength, Emperor Selassie brought Jagama back to the palace in his personal car and presented him with a gold watch and a fancy coat. Jagama helped the emperor after that, and Italy left for good later in 1941.

After the war, Jagama finally got formal soldier training and had a long, successful career in the Ethiopian Army, rising to the rank of general. He fought in other conflicts, and, though wounded several times, he lived a long life to 97.

But through all the years, perhaps this funny story best sums up who this rich farm boy became. Near the end of the Italian war, Jagama got sick with malaria and was taken to a British-run hospital in the capital. There, the British doctor refused to treat him unless he cut his afro. Jagama was proud of his hair, so he left in anger and went home. Finally, Emperor Selassie himself came to Jagama's house and ordered him to please cut his hair and get treatment for the malaria. Jagama gave in, and the doctors saved him. But he showed how stubborn he had become. He had gone into the bush as a boy and resisted an invasion. He wasn't going to give-in easily on anything, even getting a haircut.

DISCUSSION GUIDE

Review Questions:

1. Why did Italy invade Ethiopia in 1935?

2. How did the Ethiopian patriots get their weapons?

Discussion Questions:

1. Do you really think that Italy's shame from its first defeat by Ethiopia led to their leaders' fighting the country again?

2. How would you feel if another country invaded yours? What do you think you'd do?

3. Do you think guerrilla warfare — sneak attacks, hit-and-run — is fair? Why or why not?

Project Idea:

Make a radio news broadcast. Much of the news of World War II came to listeners over the radio. Write a short news report as if you're telling an audience about what was going on in Ethiopia in 1941.

- Start with a brief intro: "This is ___ reporting from Ethiopia..."

- Give a quick summary of the invasion

- Share the story of Jagama, patriot leader

- Include a key event from his story, for instance, the raid on the fort or the parade for the emperor

- Conclude with a line about the future of the emperor and hope for Ethiopia

- Extras: Record the broadcast on a phone, maybe interview friends acting as witnesses, or have them add sound effects such as screams at the raid or drums at the parade.

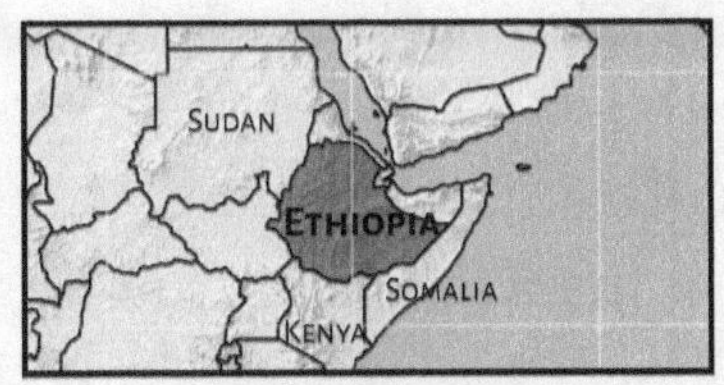

CHAPTER 14

FRANCE: JOAN OF ARC (1412-1431)

TEENAGE INSPIRATION FOR A NATION

Among the French people, a legend was told that a maiden, a young unmarried woman, would save them someday from wars and a foreign king. Many, including French leaders, now wondered, could this teenager, Joan, be the one to free France from English rule? She was so confident, so sure, but she was just a peasant girl from a small farming town. Were those prophecies, these guesses about the future, really true? And were they about her? This is the amazing history of Joan of Arc.

When Joan of Arc was born in 1412 on a farm in Domremy (pronounced DAWN-*ray-me*), France, the French had more or less been at war with England for 75 years. The horror of that war was very much a part of Joan's childhood. The people of Domremy were the victims of attacks from enemy soldiers, who stole cattle, kidnapped women and burned property. As a child, Joan found comfort in the church. She went to pray every day and *fasted* — skipped eating — as part of her faith. She was a quiet and well-behaved girl. However, when she was 13, her life took an unbelievable spiritual turn.

Joan heard a voice call her name in her father's garden one day, *I come from God to help you,* the voice said, and then, *Little Joan, be good.* Joan at first did not know where the voice was coming from. But she soon saw the angel, Saint Michael, dressed in a knight's armor with a helmet and shield. In the months and years after, Joan heard voices often and had visions of saints. Over time, they told her that she was going to lead France in the war against England and win the throne back for the French king, Charles VII. She resisted, naturally. How could she lead an army? She was just a kid! She said: *I'm a poor girl and don't know how to ride a horse or make war.* But Joan came to believe that she was the maiden from the legend shared at the start of this chapter. She had been chosen to save her country and to make Charles the king.

Historians do not know exactly what Joan saw or heard, but it's clear that she believed it, and she acted on it. Not everyone back then believed her, either. Her father told her he'd throw her in the river before he let her join the army!

But at 16, Joan was determined to meet with Charles to tell him what the voices had to told her, to do her part to make him king again. She thought the local lord (ruler) could help, so she walked more than ten miles to see him. It didn't go well. The lord told her to go home to get a beating from her dad! Still, Joan vowed she would talk to Charles even if she had to travel on her knees — the saints had commanded her.

About six months later, in 1429, she went back to the local lord, this time with a bigger reputation and more allies. At the same time, French leaders were growing desperate. The English had laid *siege* to the important French city of Orleans and were closing in on total control of France. A *siege* means the English surrounded the city and stopped supplies, such as food and weapons, from going in. So the lord finally agreed to help Joan see Charles.

When Joan went to talk to Charles, she was dressed in a boy's outfit with short hair. She was just 17 as she entered a grand hall full of important people. They had all heard about the peasant girl from Domremy who claimed to be on a mission from God. They were curious but doubted her story. To test whether she really had God on her side, Charles played a trick on her. He stood back in the crowd wearing regular clothes while other men stood forward in fancier outfits. Even though she had never seen Charles before, she found him and knelt before him. She was not fooled! The crowd started to believe. This was a big moment for Joan.

Charles hoped that Joan might inspire his army to take back the city of Orleans. He was feeling a lot of pressure from the English army, and he was out of options. So Joan was fitted with a suit of armor and given banners decorated with "Jesus" and "Mary" to show that she fought for God, not just France. Taking a leadership role with the army, Joan urged the men to stop swearing and stealing. Suddenly, other men wanted to join up — they'd heard that the army was led by a saint. Indeed, as Joan rode to battle in Orleans, she cried for God to join her, *Come, Holy Spirit!* She was a force.

When her army arrived near Orleans in April 1429, the town was in terrible shape. The siege had made the citizens hungry and scared. Joan and some men were able to sneak into the city, and her presence changed everything. She brought hope and belief to the people and confidence to the soldiers as the battle to free Orleans began. After taking two forts from the English, Joan predicted that she would be wounded above her chest. The next day, she was indeed shot by an arrow right where she'd claimed. However, legend says that she removed the arrow herself, said a prayer and returned to the battle! Joan and the French were unstoppable. Soon, the English retreated, a huge victory for France at Orleans.

Joan continued to free France over the following weeks. In July of 1429, Charles VII was crowned king of France with Joan at his side. In many ways, Joan had kept the promise made in her visions and fulfilled the prophecy of the maiden. Still, she continued to fight to remove the English from all of France, and she was eventually captured in May of 1430.

The English wanted to be rid of Joan, who had turned the war around and proved to be an inspiration for their French enemies. They put Joan on trial for breaking church rules, things like witchcraft, wearing men's clothes, and claiming to talk to God. While Joan did her best to fight back, she was not supported fairly at her trial and was found guilty and executed. France nonetheless rode Joan's spirit to take most of France back and end the war now known as the Hundred Years War by 1453. Years later, after Joan died, a new church trial found that she wasn't guilty, and the church made her a saint centuries later.

Today, you'll find statues of Saint Joan of Arc all over France. She is celebrated each year in Orleans and remembered across the country, even after the long-time peace between France and England. Perhaps no hero has ever been as purely inspiring. She stayed true to her beliefs and never quit. Just one teenager, Joan became a symbol for a nation.

DISCUSSION GUIDE

Review Questions:

1. Who did Joan talk to to help set up a meeting with Charles?

2. Why did people start to believe in her in Charles' court?

3. What kind of military strategy was England using at Orleans when Joan arrived?

Discussion Questions:

1. Have you ever had to convince someone of the truth when they didn't want to believe you? What happened? What did you do to convince them?

2. What voices do you think Joan really heard? Does it matter?

3. Do you think Joan actually made a difference in battle if she didn't always carry her sword? Why or why not?

Project Idea:

Make a Joan-Style Banner. Imagine that you need to inspire everyone around you to go out and win. You can pretend that you are a soldier leading an historic army such as Joan's or another army such as the Allies in World War II, or you can use any other competitive team occasion, such as your own soccer team or your favorite college football or basketball team.

On a piece of poster board, draw slogans and symbols to encourage your fellow soldiers or teammates to fight on to victory. Words are great, "Believe it! We can win!" "Don't ever quit!" "Give 100% all the time!" Pictures are great too – your logo, mascot, flags and symbols. When you're done you'll know a little about how Joan felt carrying her banner.

CHAPTER 15

FRANCE: LOUIS BRAILLE (1809-1852)

OPENING THE WORLD TO THOSE WITHOUT SIGHT

Starting to feel excited, the boy had to stay calm: "You can read faster," the boy told his teacher. The student was writing down what his teacher was saying, and the teacher was speaking slowly so the boy could keep up. But the boy was keeping up without a problem! Both were surprised at how fast the boy was writing. He wasn't using regular alphabet letters — he was making tiny dents in thick paper, a system of writing he had invented for kids like him, kids who were blind. While no one is sure that this is exactly what happened when he first shared his new writing system, here is the incredible true story of Louis Braille.

Louis Braille was born in 1809 in a small country village in France. He had three older siblings and often tried to keep up with them around the hills and farms of their town. Young Louis also loved messing about in his father's leather shop — his dad made saddles and harnesses and other horse-riding gear from leather.

One day, when Louis was three, he was trying to be like his dad, using a sharp tool to poke a hole in leather — he leaned down close to the strap to get it just right, like his father. But as Louis jammed the tool into the leather, the point slid off, and his eye was badly hurt. Over time his eye grew infected (germs were in the cut), and the infection spread to his other eye. By the time Louis was five years old, he was completely blind.

Because Louis was not born blind, he was sad at first and wondered why it was always so dark. He longed to play in the fields as he had before. Louis's parents also wanted him to be able to do what other boys did. They taught him to read by making the shape of letters with nails hammered into wood, so Louis could *feel* the letters. Louis was bright and curious, and his other senses strengthened when he could not see.

Louis quickly showed what a good student he was at the local school, but that school was not set up for blind students — he had to memorize lessons differently because he could not read the books. So at ten years old, Louis's parents agreed to send him to a special school for the blind in France's capital, Paris. They hated to let him go but knew this was his best chance to learn the most and lead a fuller life. What they did not know was that this was a decision that would change the world.

At the Institute for Blind Youth in Paris, a new world was opened to Louis. He made great friends and learned to play the cello and the organ. Everything was not perfect there, though. Built in a former school for priests, the Institute was cold, damp and very plain, and the students were often sick, including Louis. He missed the fresh air and countryside of his family's home. Still, the school had things he couldn't get at home. There were books with raised letters that blind children could read by tracing their fingers over the letters. But the reading was slow, with few words to a page. It made Louis want more.

In 1821, when Louis was about 12, he and his classmates were shown a new way for blind people to read. Called "sonography" or "night writing," the system used groups of 12 raised dots you could feel on paper. Louis still wanted something faster and less complicated. Using this *night writing* as a starting place, Louis began working through school breaks and free time and sickness to come up with a better way for blind people to read. He wouldn't rest because he knew that reading and writing would make everything better for his friends and classmates.

At 15, just a kid, Louis finally felt that he had come up with a system worth sharing. He showed his teacher his idea: six spots in three rows of two that could be used to make different patterns of raised dots. Each pattern was a letter (versus *night writing* where each pattern was a sound) — all 26 letters of the alphabet in different simple codes of six dots. One finger could *read* a letter all at once! Simple, fast and so smart.

The Institute's director, Alexandre-Rene Pignier, tested the writing and reading system with Louis, and it worked! Louis was faster than they'd ever been with the raised letters or *night writing*. Soon, the other kids at the Institute were using Louis's code. When a new director wanted to stop students from using it, the students refused. It was too important to them. They could write down their lessons. They could write notes to each other! It was only a matter of time before Louis's idea, now called by his last name, Braille, became the written language of blind people all over the world.

Louis's life in the early 1800s came right at the end of an era called the Enlightenment. During this time, thinkers in Europe put forth the idea that people could use science and study of the world to make it better. They believed our lives were not solely up to fate or chance. This changing attitude included the way people thought about people with disabilities. Many blind people before the Enlightenment were likely to lead a life of begging. In fact, the man who founded Louis's school, one of the first for blind students, had seen a group of blind beggars being made fun of on the street when he was young. He was so upset by it that he made it his life's goals to help and educate blind children. Louis was able to attend the Institute and invent Braille as a result of that man's Enlightenment goals. Then the Braille system was another huge step forward in improving the lives of blind people.

After graduating from the Institute, Louis became a teacher there until he died at 43 years old. He never fully recovered from the tuberculosis (a lung disease) that he caught in his 20s, but he lived a truly extraordinary life. Louis overcame the accident in his father's workshop to make a difference for all blind people — forever. A memorial at this birthplace in France speaks to his heroism. It reads: "He opened the doors of knowledge to all those who cannot see." And Louis opened those huge doors when he was just a kid.

Discussion Guide

Review Questions:

1. What did Louis's parents do to help him learn after he lost his sight?

2. Where was Louis's school for blind people, and what was good and bad about it?

3. Why was Braille better than other systems of writing and reading for blind people?

Discussion Questions:

1. Can you think of a challenge that you've overcome, a time when you were facing something that seemed hard for you but that you did anyway?

2. Do you think that France as a nation had done everything it could for blind people in setting up the Institute? Why or why not?

3. What kinds of jobs do you think blind people could do thanks to Braille that they could not do before?

Project Idea:

Write your name in Braille. The Braille alphabet may seem challenging at first. But take a look below — Louis's design is so smart. The first ten letters, A-J, have no dots raised in the bottom row. The second ten letters, K-T, have one dot in the bottom row. The last 6 letters, V-Z (except for W, which was added later), have both dots raised in the bottom row. So your finger knows immediately which group of letters you're in, making it easier to read the letter.

For a project, try writing your name in Braille. Using a ruler to keep the dots straight, make a 6-dot grid for each letter you need to spell your name. You can make them small so they're more like real braille books, or larger to be more decorative — your call. Then, using white glue from a bottle, make glue dots on each dot needed to turn a grid into a letter in your name. Let the glue dry, then close your eyes and run your fingers over the glue bumps to feel the braille letters. Decorate and hang it up!

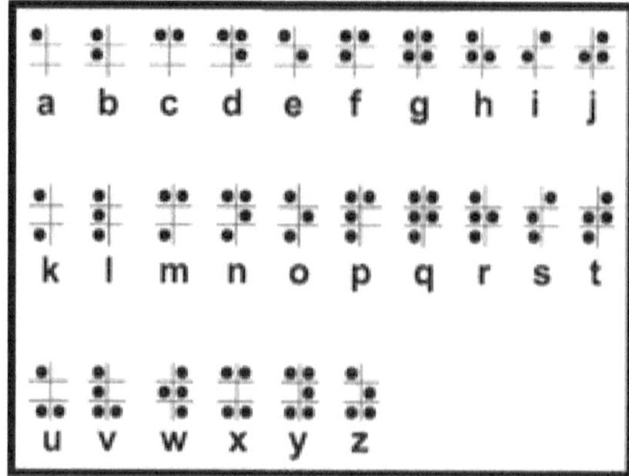

CHAPTER 16

FRANCE: BLAISE PASCAL (1623-1662)

THE BOY WHO SOLVED GROWN-UP PROBLEMS

His father was a tax collector who was constantly adding numbers in books, rows and rows of numbers added with a quill (feather) pen. This boy's mother had died, and he was very close to his dad; he boy wanted to help him with his math work. This was centuries before computers and pocket calculators. So the boy set out to create a kind of calculator, almost 400 years ago. Did he ever figure out a way to help his father? Read more about the amazing Blaise Pascal to find out.

Blaise (pronounced like BLAZE) Pascal was born in a small city in central France, the only boy in the middle of two sisters. His father, Etienne, was a tax judge, someone who looked after cases about the amount of taxes a citizen was paying. Blaise's mother died when he was about 3, shortly after his little sister was born, and when Blaise was eight, his father decided that they should move to Paris. There, the family could get more support, and the kids could enjoy greater opportunities among the educated circles of France's biggest city. Without a mom around, Blaise got very close to his dad and sisters.

A mathematician himself, Etienne educated his children at home, although at first he did not let Blaise study math. Etienne wanted his son to learn the classics — Greek and Latin, and was afraid Blaise would fall in love with math and learn nothing else if given the chance. So math became like a treat Blaise couldn't have, and, like any kid, it made him want it even more! Imagine sneaking math the way you sneak candy — that's how it was for Pascal. While secretly doing math, Blaise figured out all on his own some advanced ideas about triangles. At just 12, he showed his dad what he'd learned, and Etienne had to admit that it was no use — his son was a math whiz. Dad had to feed him numbers.

In truth, Blaise was a prodigy, a very talented child. He was to science what Mozart was to music, a natural kid-genius. At 14, Blaise was attending meetings with important mathematicians. At 16, after just a few short years of studying math, Blaise publicly presented his ideas to adults and published his first paper on geometry, the study of shapes. This essay about cones is still studied today.

It was about this time that Blaise's family moved out of Paris to northern France, where Etienne became the head of tax collection. This job meant exhausting number crunching about who owed what, who had paid what, and so on. Blaise's big brain set to work on a machine to assist his dad. When he was just 18 in 1642, Blaise invented the *Pascaline*, a kind of large calculator where you could add and subtract numbers.

It didn't work miracles, but it did help, and many consider it the world's first machine calculator. Pretty impressive for a teenager!

Blaise would go on to make incredible advances in science. From a top-of-mountain experiment in the 1640s, he figured out that air pressure goes down as you go higher. With a friend in the 1650s, he created the math of probability; this is the way people predict the chances that something will happen, like your odds of winning the lottery — we might not have huge gambling casinos without Pascal. Blaise also invented the *syringe*, used for shots and drawing blood. And he laid out a plan for public transportation — carriages that ran the same routes at the same time every day, regardless of whether there were passengers.

In many ways, Pascal was ahead of his time. His Pascaline did not sell a lot, and his public transport idea didn't take off. But he was at the center of many huge debates in his time about religion and philosophy (the study of big ideas about the meaning of life). He was a mathematician and inventor but also a serious thinker about God and humankind. In his 30s, after a dreamlike experience, he became very religious. He came to share his belief that some truths cannot be understood with step-by-step thinking but can only be answered with your heart. Blaise died likely from stomach cancer at just 39, but this "reason of the heart"

was an idea perhaps as memorable and thoughtful as any he'd published about geometry.

So what also makes Pascal such a fascinating historical figure might be the wide number of things he was involved in, and in a short life. From math to religion to transportation, his deep interest in the whole world around him is inspiring. There are other characters like him who explored diverse fields — Leonardo daVinci may come to mind, but Pascal arguably did more earlier in life than any of them, which is why he's in this book. And now you know how much you might accomplish if you just sneak a little more math.

DISCUSSION GUIDE

Review Questions:

    1. How was Pascal educated?

    2. Name three things Pascal discovered, invented or created.

Discussion Questions:

    1. Do you really think Blaise liked math more because he wasn't allowed to do it? Do you think his father knew that he would like it more?

    2. Why do you think his ideas for the Pascaline and public transit weren't more popular?

Project Idea:

Fun with Probability. Let's do two experiments with probability.

    1. Coin. If you flip a coin 20 times, how many will be heads? Go ahead and flip a coin 20 times and keep track of the results. Was it exactly what you thought? Why or why not?

    2. Dice. If you roll two dice together 40 times, what totals do you think will come up the most? Go ahead and roll the dice and keep track of the sums from 40 rolls. What totals came up the most? Why?

Having done these two experiments, do you think you can predict coin flips and dice rolls better? Do you think it's fair to decide something based on a coin flip? What about a roll of the dice — it might depend on what the rules are!

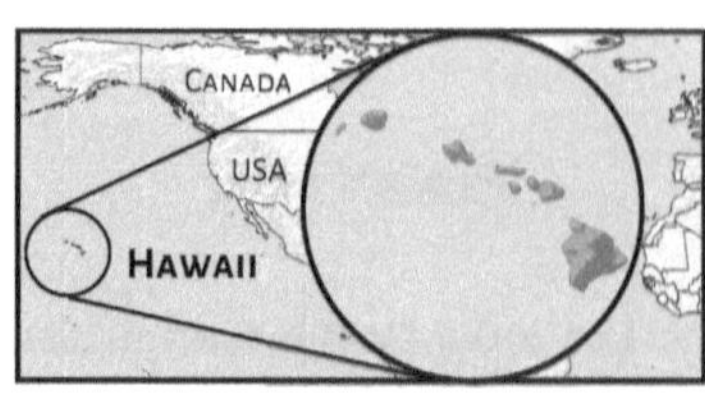

CHAPTER 17

HAWAII: JOSEPH KEKUKU (1874/5-1932)

THE KID WHO MADE THE GUITAR SING

This eleven-year-old Hawaiian boy loved to play guitar. He was good at it. One day in 1886, he was strumming the instrument when a metal comb fell out of his shirt pocket, hitting the guitar strings as it fell. The sound that it made, unlike anything he'd ever heard, was like a sad call from a bird of paradise. The new sound was rich but haunting. This boy would spend much of his life chasing and perfecting that sound. Here is the awesome story of Joseph Kekuku, the inventor of the Hawaiian steel guitar.

Hawaii (spelled Hawai'i in the Hawaiian language) was an independent kingdom when Joseph Kekuku was born on the island of Oahu in the 1870s. Joseph's parents were Native Hawaiians and part of a Mormon community including families from the U.S. The oldest of six kids, Joseph always had lots of siblings and cousins around to play music. They all fiddled with instruments that were common in their village: violin, ukulele (like a small four-string guitar) and guitar.

When he was about 11, he first came upon the sound of the steel guitar. One story of discovery told earlier in this chapter is about a steel comb falling on the strings. In another version, Joseph put down his guitar to open a package with a knife and dropped the knife on the instrument. In another, he found a railroad spike and ran it along the strings. While there are different tales about the discovery, this is clear: when he stumbled onto the sound, Joseph's love of guitar collided with his childhood wonder, and then his curiosity took over!

For years, Joseph would experiment with different metal objects that he would slide along the strings. Yes, we aren't sure which item sparked Joseph's excitement for this sound, but we know where he finished. Here's what happened. When he was about 14, he went away to school in Honolulu, Hawaii's largest city. He was smart, and he was passionate about music. But most of all, he was determined. Guitar is a challenging instrument requiring lots of practice and hand strength, but that didn't stop Joseph from mastering it and even trying to improve it. Imagine that. For almost everyone, it's enough just to learn an instrument. He wanted to make it better! So Joseph worked with his shop teacher to make a smooth, metal cylinder — about the size and shape of your pointer finger — to slide along the strings. Joseph also changed his guitar, replacing the strings with metal ones and raising them off the wood to make better sounds with his metal bar.

Simply put, Joseph had created a new instrument out of the guitar. In Joseph's method, you lay the guitar flat on your lap, plucking the strings with one hand and running a steel bar along the guitar's neck. This made a new set of sounds that could be used with traditional guitar songs but could also make brand new music no one had ever heard before. And he was just a kid!

People loved the unique sound. This new *steel guitar* became almost a human voice in Joseph's hands, a rising, falling and sliding cry that seemed to sway like Hawaii's trees in the ocean breeze. Joseph taught his schoolmates to play, and the amazing new music spread. He had his first public performance at Honolulu's Mission Memorial Auditorium when he was still just a teenager. When Joseph's parents moved to Utah for religious reasons, he stayed behind in Hawaii. He was committed to his music. The steel lap guitar was becoming the *Hawaiian style.*

At the same time, life in the Hawaiian islands was changing. In 1893, the Hawaiian Kingdom was overthrown, and the United States soon had much more control. Traditional Hawaiian ways, such as the native language and dance, were at risk of being pushed out. Soon after, maybe to save his guitar style, Joseph actually brought his Hawaiian sound to mainland America when he was 29 in 1904. At an international event in Seattle in 1909 and a 1914 World's Fair in San Francisco, millions were introduced to Joseph's music. It was an instant hit. In 1919, he started an eight-year tour of Europe with other Hawaiian musicians and performers. By the 1920s, Hawaiian music and the steel guitar were becoming known around the world.

Stepping back for a moment, Joseph was sharing his music with audiences across the U.S. and Europe, thanks to a world that was becoming easier to travel around and more urban (people living in cities). That is, steamships and railroads brought performers quickly from big city to big city. They also brought immigrants to new countries. On his tours in American cities, Joseph would stay in hotels with all kinds of people: acrobats and dancers from many countries and African-American jazz and blues players. Perhaps it's not a surprise that this mixing of people led to a mixing of musical styles. The steel guitar, over time, became a huge part of blues, country and eventually rock ' n ' roll. It can add a loneliness to blues, a lift to country and a depth to rock.

Joseph Kekuku lived a life full of music. He died in 1932. In 1993, the Steel Guitar Hall of Fame added Joseph and honored him as the inventor of the Hawaiian steel guitar. While some competing claims exist, most historians credit Joseph with the invention. Indeed, his statue at the Polynesian Cultural Center in Hawaii names him "father of the Hawaiian steel guitar."

Now if you've ever seen a play, a movie or even a television commercial set in Hawaii or other island setting, you may have heard Joseph's invention. Some songs you might know that feature the sound? Try the island Christmas classic, *Mele Kalikimaka,* or the unforgettably dreamy, *Sleep Walk.* It's a sound you probably love, and it probably makes you think of all the beauty of places like Hawaii. And it's all thanks to a kid who dropped his comb! He had the curiosity to learn more and the passion to make it happen.

DISCUSSION GUIDE

Review Questions:

1. What changes did Joseph make to his guitar and the way he played it to make it sound different?

2. What kinds of music feature Joseph's instrument today?

Discussion Questions:

1. Did you know that the Hawaiian sound was a steel guitar? Can you think of other items - instruments or others - that local people changed to make their own, reinventing something arriving from elsewhere?

2. Why do you think there are different versions of how Joseph

discovered the sound? Which one do you think is the right one? Does it matter?

Project Ideas:

1. **Slide Sound Sleuth**. If you have an old guitar around that your parents won't mind you messing with, this is a fun project. If not, try number 2 below. For this project, you'll need the guitar and three smooth metal objects, for example, a spoon, a metal ruler and a dull tool like a Phillips head screwdriver. Put the guitar on your lap, strings up. Pluck a guitar string and lightly slide one of the objects along the string on the neck of the guitar. Try it slowly and then quickly and note the change in sound. As a bonus, you can name the sounds, for instance, "baby cry" or "whale song." Try each object and figure out which one sounds the most musical and clear. Now you know what Joseph did!

2. **Invent an Instrument**. Try drawing a new instrument by thinking of an existing instrument and then adding something that the instrument doesn't do today, such as making an echo or an animal sound. Draw the updated instrument and label the new parts. Share your dream!

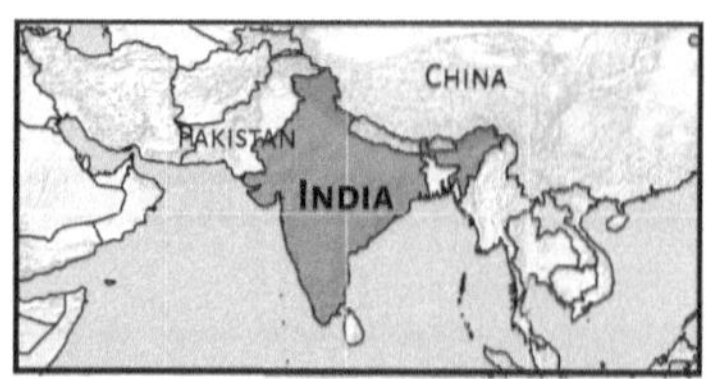

CHAPTER 18

INDIA: SAVITRIBAI PHULE (1831-1897)

THE GIRL WHO TAUGHT GIRLS

It's a usual weekday morning in the closely packed houses and shops in the old neighborhoods of Pune, a city in western India. A very young teacher, just 17, is walking to the small school where little girls are her students. As she turns down a busy, narrow lane, smack! A loose ball of mud hits her right in the cheek. Brushing it off with the back of her hand, the dirt smears on the sleeve of her sari, her traditional Indian dress. She doesn't stop to see who threw it. She doesn't even slow down. But then she stumbles as a thrown stone hits her in the back, right between her shoulders. She grinds her teeth, fighting back tears, but keeps going. As she arrives at her school, the girls run smiling to greet her; she lets out a breath and goes to clean herself up. This is just a day in the life of the brave educator, Savitribai Phule (pronounced suh-VEE-tree-bye POO-lay). Let's read her courageous story.

Savitribai wasn't supposed to know how to read or write. Born into a poor farming family in western India in 1831, most people in her village didn't think girls needed an education. It was the tradition in her village for very young girls to be married by their families and to go live with the husbands' families. At just 9 years old, Savitribai was married to Jyotirao (pronounced JOE-*tee-rou*) Phule and sent to grow up with her husband's family. She'd never had a day of school.

But she was curious about Jyotirao's books. While most girls were focused on learning cooking and sewing, Savitribai wanted to read and write. She worked on the family farm during the day and studied at home whenever she could. Even though she was not allowed to go to school in her village, Savitribai was a passionate student. Also, Savitribai and Jyotirao had big ideas about educating the poor. These ideas upset the family. Savitribai's father-in-law finally told them to leave his house. So she and her husband set up life on their own in the nearby city of Pune when they were only teenagers.

Determined to keep learning, Savitribai kept studying at home. She eventually joined a teacher-training class run by an American missionary (a person who travels to other countries to spread a religion). Savitribai learned quickly. At just 16, she passed her exams to become a teacher, the first female in modern India! What did she want to do with all her knowledge? Why share it with other girls, of course! Savitribai, her husband and a friend opened a small school for girls in 1848, the first school for girls in the city.

But it wasn't that easy. The family structure that Savitribai was part of in India — the young marriages arranged by families — might not work if the girls were going to school and getting bigger ideas about what they wanted to do. Many people living around the school did not want girls to learn, and they let Savitribai know it, even though she was only a teenager. Every day as she walked to the school to teach, people would throw rocks and mud and even cow dung at her. They called her names and screamed insults. Imagine having to leave your house to go to work every day, knowing that you were going to face that. Most people would get a different job. Not Savitribai. In fact, she just wore a dirty sari every day and packed a clean one. Smart, right? She would let them throw mud at her dirty dress, then change into a new one when she got to school. Just part of the job, she told herself.

Young Savitribai cared deeply about girls' education and was determined to give Indian girls more opportunities. Getting insulted on the street was a small price to pay to help open doors for future Indian women. With her fiery strength, her school thrived. Just a few girls at first from poor families, the school grew. She went door to door telling parents why their girls needed an education, that girls could help their families with money and communications if they got schooling. And Savitribai taught modern stuff, including math, science and history. They opened three more schools. By the time she was about 20, Savitribai was running three schools for girls in Pune with 150 students! When she was about 21, she won an award for the best teacher in the whole region.

India in the mid-1800s was going through a lot of big changes. Your life in India, in many ways, had been set by the level of wealth you were born into, your *caste*. Also, British rule in India had limited the leadership and rights of Indians in their own country. At the same time, the British had brought a modern worldview to India, opening the eyes of many to aim higher than what the *caste system* said. Savitribai was a fighter for poor women at a time when women in India were just starting to understand the possibilities of equality, and education was a huge first step. She gave families hope that their daughters could have more choices.

We've discussed what Savitribai did as a kid, but as she aged, she did not stop at teaching and starting schools. She opened a shelter for women in the 1850s. In 1873, she and Jyotirao started a group called the Truth-Seekers' Society that worked for fair treatment for people from every caste. What really makes Savitribai so special as a changemaker is that she always *did* what she argued for. That is, she did more than protest to make a difference. She also gave her own time and sweat. For example, when she wanted to help poor Indians get access to clean water, she dug a drinking well in her own yard!

In her 60s, when a deadly sickness swept through her city, she went out herself to help the sick. One day, she carried a very ill boy from a poor part of town to get aid. While the boy survived, Savitribai herself caught the illness and died in 1897. Just like when she was a teenager and let the world throw mud at her, she took on the disease herself. Savitribai was a real-life hero in history, and she got all her training showing courage as a kid.

DISCUSSION GUIDE

Review Questions:

1. What *firsts* did Savitribai accomplish in education?

2. What examples in Savitribai's life show how she was willing to do herself what she wanted India to do for less fortunate citizens?

Discussion Questions:

1. How do you think families decided to send their daughters to Savitribai's school? What do you think they saw as the risks and rewards?

2. Why did Savitribai get help from an American missionary? What role do you think foreigners played in Savitribai's becoming a fighter for women's rights?

Project Idea:

Roleplay at the home of a potential student. Act out a short scene where Savitribai and her team knock on the door of a home of a family with school-age girls. One or two people are Savitribai and a partner, and one or two people are a parent or parents of a daughter.

- Scene opens with a knock and answer at a door

- Savitribai's team explains their mission; they've opened a school for girls and ask about school-age girls in the house and their current education

- Parent team explains their position on education and why their daughters don't attend

- Parent team asks questions and shares concerns

- Savitribai's team shares benefits of education and why knowing more actually makes girls better wives and moms

- Teams part with some resolution to come back or visit the school

CHAPTER 19

IRAN: ISMAIL I (1487-1524)

THE BOY WHO BUILT A NATION

*B*efore the battle started, it was quiet. The 14-year-old boy sat on his horse and gazed at a much bigger army across the battlefield. These were the same enemies that had killed his father years before. Now this teenager was leading an army of grown men against them. Many of the men he led were old enough to be his father. He probably shouted, "We fight so that our people can stand together as one!" Then with a loud cheer behind him, he charged his horse first into the Battle of Sharur in 1501. Even though his army was much smaller, they won, and the road to the great city ahead was now open. This is the story of Ismail I, the shah (ruler) of Iran.

Ismail was born in 1487 into a powerful family in the mountains of northern Iran, in a region historians often call Persia. His family led a religious group of Muslims (followers of Islam) called the Safavids (pronounced SAH-*fuh-vids*). The Safavids began as a religious group known for prayer and teaching. By Ismail's time, they also had tough fighters who followed them.

The Safavids had many enemies who fought them for control of land in Persia. When Ismail was very young, his father was killed in battle. Those who still believed in the Safavid cause were afraid that the same enemies would try to wipe out Ismail's whole family. They decided that if Ismail was going to survive to lead them someday, he had to go into hiding. When he was seven, they moved him far away to a secret home near the Caspian Sea. Growing up there, teachers taught him the prayers and stories of the Safavids and the legend of his own father. Young Ismail was handed a very heavy load: grief for his dad, the promise to get back at his dad's enemies and the need to take back the land for his people.

But Ismail could handle it. In many ways, he was special. First, he looked unusual. A visitor from Italy wrote that Ismail had reddish hair, in a country where dark hair was more common, so he stood out in a crowd. The same visitor said that Ismail didn't just look different, *he was different*. He was stronger and braver than others and awesome at archery — hitting seven of ten apples in a contest, and he was left-handed.

Now you might expect that kids grew up faster in 1400s Persia than kids today. And that's true. But that usually meant doing more work on farms, helping in a market or learning a trade. Some royal children even became kings or queens at a young age, but they usually had adults around to make the big decisions. Ismail's story is not like that. When he was only 12, he came out of hiding to take his father's former place as leader of the Safavids. Older army leaders and families around Iran came to him and promised to fight for him. They believed he was chosen by God to lead them. Some experienced leaders helped with the Safavids' plans, but young Ismail was the face and heart of everything.

With more followers and soldiers pledged to him, Ismail rode south with an army of red-hatted warriors. They won battles at Shirvan and other cities where people had sided against the Safavids. The first really big victory was at Sharur, which was described in the opening of this chapter. After that, Ismail confidently marched into the rich city of Tabriz and crowned himself shah of Iran. His message was clear — *we are going to create a new land ruled by a local king, not by distant warlords.* He was only 14!

Ismail continued to lead his army to expand their territory, winning battle after battle and getting revenge for his father. He did ruthless and shocking things to scare his rivals, like turning a defeated rival's skull into a decorated cup. Though as shah, Ismail was not solely a fighter. He also wrote poems in simple, everyday language that his followers could sing and memorize. The poems praised God, loyalty, and Ismail's special mission, helping people see him as a kind of holy leader, not just a king. He also announced that a branch of Islam, Shi'a (pronounced SHE-*ah*) Islam would be the official religion of his new state. In many places prayers in mosques changed, teachers arrived to spread Shi'a beliefs, and some people who refused to go along were punished, losing jobs, homes or worse. Ismail wanted everyone together under one faith, but making that happen caused pain and anger too.

After more than a decade of victories on battlefields, young Ismail seemed to be unbeatable. He had conquered much of northern and western Iran. But further to the west was the powerful Ottoman Empire. By his mid-20s, Ismail was getting a lot of angry letters from the Ottoman sultan, who threatened Ismail with war, saying that he was too powerful and dangerous to their faith. Ismail answered with less anger, almost teasing, *I thought we were friends!* But he closed his letter firmly, writing that they'd quickly go to battle if needed. And they did.

In 1514, at the Battle of Chaldiran, Ismail's forces fought the Ottomans, and Ismail was finally crushed in defeat. The Ottomans simply had better weapons: new guns and cannons and more soldiers. Ismail escaped, but he never quite got back his swagger. He became depressed and, over time, led troops into fewer and fewer battles. He died in 1524.

But Ismail had already dared to lead older, more experienced people. He had successfully started an empire that would last more than 200 years. Historians credit that dynasty with helping to form modern Iran, setting up shah rule with strong central leadership, supporting arts and education, and making Persia an important trading bridge between Europe and Asia. Over time, Safavid rulers controlled lands reaching north into what is now Russia, west to Turkey, east into Pakistan, and south to the Persian Gulf. Many of Iran's modern borders grew from the lands first united under Ismail. None of that would have started without a bold, red-haired boy who carried the weight of his family's past and fought bravely — and sometimes harshly — for their future.

DISCUSSION GUIDE

Review Questions:

1. Where did Ismail go as a child to escape his father's enemies?

2. What made Ismail different?

Discussion Questions:

1. Why do you think people followed him when he was only 12? What did those people believe? Do you think a 12-year-old could gather followers today?

2. Ismail seemed to be crushed by the defeat at the hands of the Ottomans. Why do you think that happened? Could it have been avoided?

Project Idea:

Write a letter to Ismail. Pick a time in Ismail's life, such as when he's eight in hiding, when he's 12 coming out of hiding, after the Battle of Sharur, after he makes his branch of religion official, or after the Battle of Chaldiran. Next, pick your role as writer - are you an advisor, a citizen, a soldier or a teacher? Then give him advice:

- What should he do next?

- How should he treat people on his team?

- What about people who disagree with him?

- What should he remember about being a leader?

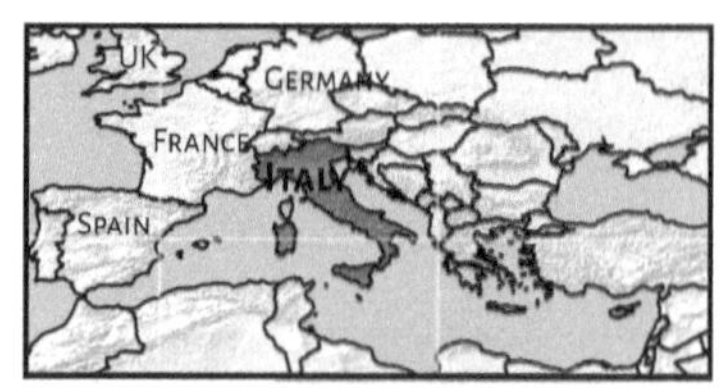

CHAPTER 20

ITALY: MICHELANGELO (1475-1564)

BORN WITH HANDS FOR STONE

He hadn't been studying art there as long as the other teenagers. But he had learned quickly and was earning more money for his artworks, and the man who paid for them seemed to like him best. One day, when the boys were wrestling around, his friend, feeling jealous of him, took the chance to punch him — really hard! — right in the nose. His nose was smashed flat for the rest of his long life! This is the story of the artist, Michelangelo (and his nose!). Why did he make his friends so jealous? Find out in this chapter.

Michelangelo (the "ch" is said like a "k" in *kite*) Buonarroti was born in 1475 into a family that was related to past royalty in Florence, Italy. At least that's what the family believed. Perhaps because of that belief, Michelangelo's father did not think his family should do work with their hands, work such as art! But the truth was that they did not have much money as a family anymore.

When Michelangelo was just 6, his mother died, and his dad sent him to live with a nanny and her husband, a stonecutter. Stonecutters dug valuable rocks, such as marble, out of the ground from *quarries* to make fine buildings and, sometimes, fine art, or *sculptures*. These early years helped carve Michelangelo's personality forever, creating his love for sculpting. He later said that the "pure air" of stonecutter country gave him "any intelligence" he ever had! In fact, for much of his life he signed his letters, "Michelangelo, Sculptor."

Seeing that Michelangelo was a smart boy, at age 10 his father brought him back to the city of Florence to attend school, which most children did not in those days. But Michelangelo was far more interested in skipping school and going to draw the beauty of Florence. He went to churches and monuments and hung around with older artists, copying *frescoes*, paintings on walls. Michelangelo's father tried to stop him, punishing him severely for choosing art over school. But it was no use. Michelangelo was determined, and at age 13 his dad agreed to have him *apprenticed* — to learn from someone skilled — to a well-known local painter, Domenico Ghirlandaio.

He was older than other apprentices starting with Ghirlandaio, but he showed such talent that he was paid for his work faster than others. Early on, he showed his boldness and confidence by correcting a copy of Ghirlandaio's painting of a woman, making it better than his teacher had. His teacher said this about one of Michelangelo's quick sketches,

"This boy knows more about it than I do"! Michelangelo had such a passion for drawing at that young age that he bought dead fish to copy the colors of their scales and stained his copies of old drawings to make them look truly old.

But his true passion was sculpture. At 15, he and some other apprentices were invited to sculpt at the Florentine palace for the city's lord (leader), Lorenzo de Medici. Michelangelo carved a faun, a fairytale creature with legs of a goat and the upper body of a man. His faun was supposed to be old, but when Lorenzo saw it, he remarked that the faun couldn't be old with so many teeth still in place. Feeling proud, Michelangelo *bang!* knocked out a tooth from the fawn's mouth. Lorenzo was impressed with Michelangelo's courage and skill. Lorenzo requested that Michelangelo live and train at the palace as if he were one of Lorenzo's sons, a huge honor. This was his big chance.

Michelangelo's work with Lorenzo really set him apart in history from other young artists who showed promise as kids. By the time he was just 17, Michelangelo had sculpted at least two museum-worthy pieces that are still loved today. The first was *Madonna of the Stairs*, a marble relief (a carving on a flat background) of the baby Jesus on his mother's lap. About the size of a poster, the carving was called "unique." The next was *Battle of the Centaurs*, a twisting, chaotic (wild) carving of 25 bodies that showed the movement and detailed human forms that Michelangelo had mastered in his earlier sketches. But these people were in rock, not ink! About the size of two large posters, the *Battle of the Centaurs* announced to Florence the presence of a rising star.

It was this outstanding talent and bold work — and some say his difficult personality and harsh attitude! — that made others jealous and got him punched in the nose. Indeed, Michelangelo showed from a young age that he was not going to be another member of his family who failed to live up to their past glory. No way. Sadly, Lorenzo died in 1492 when Michelangelo was just 17, and he had to start over in Bologna and then Rome. But within a decade, Michelangelo would be famous.

Michelangelo lived a very long life, 89 years, during a time known as the Renaissance, which means *rebirth*. It was a period from the 1400s to 1600s when Europe was coming out of the Middle Ages to embrace art and learning. Italy, especially Florence and Rome, was the center of the Renaissance, marked by a newfound belief in human creation in art, science, exploration of the globe, printing books, and even business.

You've probably heard of other well-known Renaissance artists, such as Leonardo da Vinci, but Michelangelo is considered by many to be the greatest of them. His painting on the ceiling of the Sistine Chapel in Rome and his sculpture *David* — the shepherd from the Bible who killed Goliath — still draw thousands of visitors every day! But amazingly, the passion Michelangelo found and the artwork he produced as a teenager predicted his greatness before he even turned 18.

<h3 style="text-align:center">DISCUSSION GUIDE</h3>

Review Questions:

1. When did Michelangelo first see stone cutting?

2. What was one of the best examples of his early sculpting as a teenager?

3. What was one of his best-known artworks from his adult life?

Discussion Questions:

1. Do you think your parents would approve of your wanting to be an artist? Why or why not?

2. Have you ever wished you were as good at something as one of your friends? How did you react? What did you do?

Project Idea:

Make a painting that *looks old*, just like Michelangelo did. Using a standard 8.5x11-inch sheet of paper, tear slowly and carefully along each edge. Keep the tearing close to the edge to end up with a slightly smaller, yet still rectangular, canvas for your art.

Next, use black paint (not watercolor) or ink to draw something that will remind the viewer of something old, such as a church, temple or portrait (face and shoulders) of someone in formal clothes. You could also copy a map!

Once the painting is dry, use a small amount of dark coffee to cover the paper, either with a brush or a paper towel. **NOTE: Be sure to do this over a surface that won't stain, such as a steel sink or outdoor surface — coffee stains** (that's the point!). The paper will turn brown and look aged. You can make the paper as brown as you like with darker — or more — coffee.

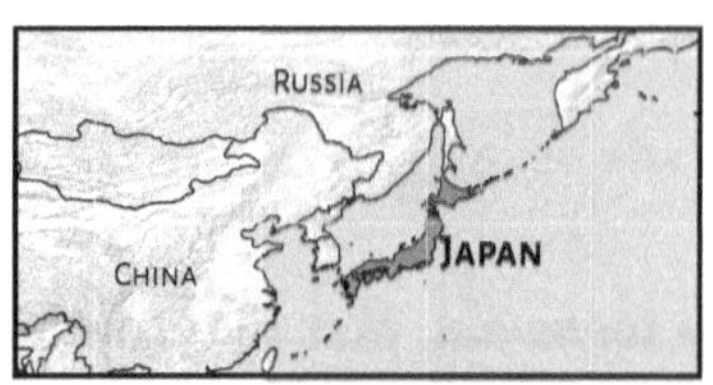

CHAPTER 21

JAPAN: SADAKO SASAKI (1943-1955)

MAKING PAPER CRANES FOR PEACE

There is an old Japanese legend about a magical bird, the crane. Some say that the crane lives 1,000 years, and if you make 1,000 paper cranes — one for every year of its life, it will grant you a wish. Any wish. When young Sadako heard about this legend, she was very sick in the hospital. She wanted to get well, to go home to her family, to run with her friends. Maybe this crane's wish could be her cure? So she started making paper cranes whenever she had the strength. Hundreds of them. Little did Sadako know then that her cranes would become a legend too. Here's what happened...

The Second World War was fought by nations all over the globe. Millions of soldiers were killed, but so were millions of ordinary people. The war in the Pacific Ocean started when Japan attacked the United States at Pearl Harbor, Hawaii, in 1941. For the next few years, the Americans and Japanese battled on and around islands all over the Pacific.

By 1945, the U.S. had created the atomic bomb, a new weapon more deadly and powerful than any before in history. American planes dropped two atomic bombs on Japanese cities, including one on Hiroshima (pronounced *he-roh-SHE-muh*), where Sadako Sasaki (pronounced *sah-DAH-koe sah-SAH-kee*) was a two-year-old girl. The death and destruction in those cities helped convince the Japanese emperor to surrender days later, ending World War II in the Pacific.

In Hiroshima, Sadako and her family were mostly able to go about their daily lives during the war. But everything changed the day the atomic bomb was dropped. Her grandmother was killed. Her home was destroyed. They fled in a small, crowded boat as the city burned. Sadako's mom and dad and her older brother survived, but when they came back, their home, neighborhood and school were in ruins. As they slowly rebuilt their community, there was little food, and, Sadako learned quickly, very little money for her family.

Growing up in Hiroshima after World War II, Sadako was known for a few special things. First, she was *brave*. Once during hide-and-go-seek, she fell out of a window and cut her head. She got stitches and barely complained.

Next, she was quick and flexible, so much so that they sometimes called her *Monkey* at school! She was the *fastest* kid in her class. In fact, in elementary school, she ran on her class's relay team. In a big school race, she got the baton just behind the leading runner and passed him before the finish line to win the race! She was kind of a class hero for that.

And Sadako was *unselfish*. Like many kids who lived through the bombing and rebuilding, she was grateful for what she had. She knew how much worse things could be. Still, there was one thing she wanted: a *kimono*, a fancy Japanese silk dress.

When Sadako was 12 years old in 1955, her aunt noticed some lumps around her neck. Her parents took her to the doctor, and they did some tests. Then more tests. Doctors in Hiroshima had seen this before — they called it A-*bomb disease*. Sadly, you know it as cancer, and doctors believed it was likely caused by the atomic bomb. Atomic weapons create radiation, poisonous rays that can cause cancer. Now, even 10 years after the bomb, Sadako was still in danger.

She was in and out of the hospital for months. The medicine they had at the time could help, but it could not cure her. Sadako's parents loved her so much; they tried to protect her from the scariest parts and keep her hopeful. Desperate to make their little girl happy, they bought her a beautiful kimono with cherry blossoms on the silk. It worked. She adored it

In the hospital, Sadako was known for being fun and friendly. She shined her flashlight through the window at a boy down the hall. She also told everyone about her goal to make 1,000 paper cranes to make a wish. Because her family had so little money, Sadako used any paper she could get her hands on. The nurses helped her collect candy packaging, gift wrap, anything. She made most of her cranes small to conserve paper, about the size of the wrapper on a piece of gum.

Sadako made hundreds of cranes, and many accounts say she made more than 1,000. But tragically, she continued to get sicker. Her parents wanted to try everything to cure her, but medicine cost a lot. Her father even sold his watch. It was no use. The cancer from the bomb weakened her to the point that the doctors did not think she would live much longer. Everyone came to see her. Her classmates missed their speedy friend and visited to say goodbye. Her teachers went to the hospital too. When she died at just 12 years old, her family was with her. Grateful to the end, some say her last quiet words were to say *thank you.*

After Sadako died, her father found notes she'd kept under her bed showing that she had known how sick she was, even if her parents didn't tell her everything. Bravely, she hardly ever asked for help. Unselfishly, some accounts say she even turned down pain medicine so her family wouldn't spend money on something that couldn't cure her.

Perhaps because of all her special traits, Sadako's schoolmates wanted her life — and the lives of other children like her — to be remembered. They had an idea. They hoped to build a memorial so that people would never forget the horror of bombs and war that had killed so many young people. The Children's Peace Monument was completed in 1958 in Hiroshima Peace Memorial Park. It's a statue of a girl like Sadako standing on a tall base, holding a golden paper crane high above her head.

Today, Sadako's memory lives on as kids around the world make paper cranes and send them to the Monument in Hiroshima to ask for peace. About 10 million cranes arrive every year! Thanks to Sadako, the world surely hears this call written on the base of the statue: "This is our cry. This is our prayer. Peace in the World."

DISCUSSION GUIDE

Review Questions:

    1. What were some of the qualities that made Sadako a special girl?

    2. How big was the paper she usually used for the cranes?

    3. Who wanted to build the monument for Sadako?

Discussion Questions:

    1. If you were Sadako's mom or dad, how would you help her

stay hopeful? Would you tell her everything?

2. Why do you think children send cranes from all over the world? What feelings and ideas in this story make kids care so much?

Project Ideas:

1. **Try your hand at origami, the Japanese art of paper folding**. I don't have room for all the illustrations needed to show how to make a crane, and it's not easy to make. But you can find directions for making a paper crane here: https://www.nps.gov/articles/000/o rigami-cranes.htm. This project will help you understand how much care Sadako had to put into her project. You might even want to send one to Hiroshima.

2. **Make a "wish for the world" postcard**. To capture the spirit of the Children's Peace Monument, take an index card and write your wish for the world on the lined side, for example, peace, health, happiness, a chicken in every pot or a puppy on every lap — your call! Then, on the blank side, draw a picture of the wish: a happy family, a peace sign, a litter of puppies. Send it to a grandparent — he or she will love it.

CHAPTER 22

KOREA: YU GWAN-SUN (1902-1920)

A STUDENT WHO TOOK A STAND

As she stood at the top of the mountain in the dark, she looked down at her hometown below, thinking about all the changes she hoped for. Then the cold March wind blew her hair over her eyes. She shielded her face and knelt down to strike a match. The wind came again, blowing out the match just as it lit. She struck another, this time carefully protecting the flame as the wind stung her cheeks. Dark, cold and wind could not stop her from lighting the signal fire on top of Mount Maebong. This 16-year-old girl was a force. Her signal fire helped tell thousands of Koreans to come to a protest the next morning. And it let many thousands more know that the fire for freedom was now burning brightly in their country. This is the story of young Korean freedom fighter, Yu Gwan-sun (pronounced YOO GWAHN-soon).

To understand the impact of Yu Gwan-sun, you need to hear about what was going on in Korea during her childhood. When Yu was a little girl in 1910, the neighboring country of Japan took control of Korea. That meant that Japan chose the leaders and laws for Korea, and it also meant that the language and customs of Koreans were being replaced by those of Japan. For example, important Korean historic buildings were torn down; parents had to give children Japanese-style names, and soldiers from Japan enforced their rules in Korean cities and towns. Many people in Korea wanted to fight back.

Yu was born in a small farming town in central Korea in 1902. Her parents were religious Christians and raised her to be the same. Yu surprised grown-ups with her ability to memorize parts of the *Bible*. At a time when most girls in Korea did not get a formal education past a young age, she won a spot at a Christian girls' school in the big city of Seoul (rhymes with *goal*). She left home to attend the school at 12.

At school, Yu became passionate about Korea's struggle for independence from Japan and joined up with other girls who wanted to help the fight. When Yu was 16, the mood in Korea changed, and students in Seoul were at the center of historic events. First, the former emperor of Korea died. Many Koreans blamed Japan and thought that the Japanese had poisoned him, even though that was not proven. When he died, the emperor did not have power anymore since the Japanese takeover, but he was still an important part of Korea's national pride, and people were furious. On March 1, 1919, not long after his funeral, thousands of people gathered to hear a reading of the Korean Declaration of Independence.

Peaceful rallies went on all day. Students spread the message of the Declaration, and Yu was part of it. This day of marches and all the related protests became known in Korea as the March First Movement.

Four days later, Yu and some of her school friends marched again in Seoul. They were taken by Japanese police, but her teachers convinced the police to let them go. The student outrage was growing. So the following week, to stop the protests, Japan ordered many schools closed, including Yu's. She would have to go back to her parents' house in the country. But before she left the city, she made a bold move; she hid a copy of the Declaration of Independence in her stuff. She was planning to bring the spirit of the protests to her village. Imagine if everyone had Yu's energy and determination.

Back in her hometown, Yu became a leader at just 16. She went door to door with the Declaration, telling her neighbors about Korea's power to be free again. She and other leaders organized a protest. They lit a signal fire the night before to alert the countryside, as shared at the beginning of this chapter. The next morning, thousands came. The rally was peaceful, but the Japanese response was not. As protestors chanted "Long live Korean independence!" Japanese soldiers shot at the crowd.

Nineteen people died, including, tragically, Yu's own mom and dad. Yu was arrested. It was April 1, 1919.

Japanese soldiers tried to get Yu to tell them who the other protest leaders were. They even offered to go easy on her if she shared their secrets. She bravely refused. She had already lost her parents; she wasn't going to give them any more. Yu was sentenced to three years in prison. She was still a teenager.

On the anniversary of the March 1 rallies, Yu helped organize a protest at the prison. Seeing her as a troublemaker, the Japanese tried to keep young Yu away from other inmates. Alone with no one to help, she was beaten by the guards over and over. She wrote: "[If] my legs and arms are crushed, this physical pain does not compare to the pain of losing my country." She died in prison in 1920. She was just 17.

Today, Koreans see Yu as a hero. Although the March First Movement did not get rid of Japan's rule, it helped establish a will to resist and a national pride in Korea that never went away. Yu is a symbol of that strength because she never gave in. In many ways, she only got stronger as she was punished and the resistance grew! After World War II in 1945, Korea was freed from Japan, although the country was divided into two independent nations, North Korea and South Korea. In 1972, a shrine (like a small temple) was built to honor Yu in her hometown. Years later, a bronze statue was added showing Yu holding up a flag and shouting for independence. She never carried a weapon or went to war, but she has been called Korea's Joan of Arc, and she is honored as a kid who lit a lasting flame for Korean freedom.

DISCUSSION GUIDE

Review Questions:

1. For about how long did Japan rule Korea?

2. What did Yu do that made her a leader and more than just a protester?

Discussion Questions:

1. What do we know about Yu's childhood that may have made her more likely to rally for independence?

2. Do you think Japanese authorities were afraid of Yu's power even though she was only a teenager? Do you think they were correct in their thinking?

Project Idea:

Make a sign to protest occupation. Think about the things that would matter most to you if you lived in a place that another country was controlling. Maybe it would be freedom or independence or your language, schools or historic places. Create a poster with a message — a slogan — about independence or your rights that you could bring to a rally to defend the things you thought were most important. Decorate with flags, symbols (peace, liberty) and positive images.

CHAPTER 23

MEXICO: TERESA URREA (1873-1906)

THE GIRL WHO HEALED HER PEOPLE

They lined up in the desert, sometimes hundreds a day, just for a chance to sit and pray with this teenage girl. Her touch, they said, had the power to heal. Little Teresa – Teresita — was just 16 when she became famous for her ability to cure people, and she became known as the young Santa de Cábora. Thousands of sick people came to see her. Many of them were poor Native Mexicans. But soon after that, Teresa was said to be "the most dangerous girl in Mexico" and sent away to the United States. What? A "dangerous"... healer? How could that be? Read more to find out!

Teresa Urrea was born into two worlds, and she may not ever have felt she fully belonged in either. Her father, Tomás Urrea, was a well-off rancher. His family came from Spain. But her mother, Cayetana Chávez, was a poor Native Mexican. Teresa's parents were not married. She and her mom lived on her father's cattle ranch in Sinaloa, Mexico. Teresa had some schooling, learning to read by age nine. Later she taught herself to write with her finger in the dust. Perhaps most importantly, an old Native woman, a *curandera* (healer) who worked on the ranch, shared her craft of traditional herbal medicine with Teresa. Teresa's skills in reading, writing and healing would change her life.

Starting when Teresa was three, the government of Mexico was run by a dictator, Porfirio Díaz, who did not allow the Mexican people to criticize his leadership. Power and wealth were limited to a few fortunate friends of Díaz. Teresa's father was not one of those friends. After supporting one of Diaz's opponents, Tomás had to leave the area — he took his ranch, his workers and Teresa's family to Cábora, a quiter place close to the U.S. border and away from Tomás's enemies.

In 1889, Teresa became very sick. She was asleep or in a kind of trance for more than three months. She said weird things and behaved differently. Then she surprised everyone and got better, but she had changed. She was more serious. Her recovery was seen as a miracle, and she believed that she needed to share that miracle. In one case, a woman with bleeding inside her chest came to see Teresa. Teresa is said to have promised, "I am going to cure you with the blood from my heart." Then she used her spit and blood and dirt to make a paste. She rubbed the paste on the woman's back, and they say she was cured.

Word spread quickly. Wagonloads of pilgrims (people on a special journey with a purpose) came with relatives who were frail, blind or paralyzed to see this wondrous girl in the high desert. Teresa would hold the sick person's hands in hers and pray. She gave hope to those in despair. She made believers out of doubters. They called this 16-year-old girl the Saint of Cábora.

Once again, Teresa was part of two worlds, one of everyday life and one of religious miracles. She may have been young, but she knew what she wanted to do. She was grateful for her ability to heal and tried to see as many people as she could. Teresa gave religious speeches about justice for the poor, and she refused to take any money for her help. To those in Cábora, it seemed that God had given power to someone like them, someone who, in Diaz's Mexico, had been powerless.

Teresa's whole story was inspiring — so inspiring that she became a hero bigger than her medicine. As rebels began to fight Diaz in Mexico, they could be heard shouting, fighting for her name: "Viva La Santa Cábora!" *Long live the Saint of Cábora!* She had become a symbol of their struggle. And for that, the Mexican government decided that Teresa was dangerous. Her family was exiled (forced to move out) from Mexico and sent to the United States in 1892. She was still just a teenager!

In the U.S., Teresa continued to lay her hands on people to heal them. She lived in Arizona, Texas and California, never settling too far from Mexico or from the events shaping her home country. She toured the U.S. performing cures before dying young at 33 in Arizona from tuberculosis (a dangerous lung disease) in 1906. The Mexican Revolution, which would remove Díaz, began just four years later.

Whether or not Teresa wanted to start a revolution remains unknown, but that mystery still tells us something important. That is, throughout history, children have become symbols for justice or change or power, and in some ways, kids make great symbols. Think about it: they aren't old enough to have made big mistakes. And their hearts are pure: they're often too young to want money or control or anything else except what they're fighting for. Teresa's story therefore teaches us that kids can sometimes change history in ways they didn't even plan themselves.

DISCUSSION GUIDE

Review Questions:

1. Why did Teresa's father move to Cábora?

2. Why did the Díaz government think Teresa was dangerous?

Discussion Questions:

1. Do you think Teresa really performed miracles or just knew good medicine, or both?

2. What other kids can you name that are or were symbols of movements? Did they ask for that role?

3. How do you think learning to read and write helped Teresa?

4. Do you think she really wanted to start a rebellion against Díaz's forces?

Project Idea:

Set up a spa. Get a small sense of the healing atmosphere that brought pilgrims to Teresa. Find a client (hint: any parent would be happy to be your client). Here are some ideas and steps:

1. Turn on soothing music - most playlist services have spa stations. If you have a radio, find the local classical music station.

2. Prepare area. Put towels on a couch and on the floor in front of the couch.

3. Prepare two large bowls of warm water for hands.

4. Soak hands for five minutes. Remove hands from bowls; dry with thick towel.

5. Apply lotion to hands.

6. Prepare bucket(s) of warm water for feet - usually, small laundry soaking tubs work.

7. Soak feet for five minutes. Remove feet from buckets; dry with thick towel.

8. Apply lotion to feet.

9. Gently wash face with lightly soaped, warm-water wash-cloth.

10. Dry face with soft towel.

11. Apply lotion to face, avoiding eyes, nose, and mouth.

12. Brush hair.

13. Clean up towels and water receptacles.

14. Listen to thanks and praise from client!

CHAPTER 24

THE NETHERLANDS: ANNE FRANK (1929-1945)

HER DIARY BECAME HISTORY

A policeman had left a terrifying note at the door. It said that Anne's sister, Margot, who had turned 16, had been called to the Nazi labor camps. But these were work camps often became places people died. Anne's parents were not going to let Margot go. They couldn't. They might never see her again. So they had only one option. The next morning, Anne, Margot and their parents wore as many clothes as they could and went into hiding. For 761 days, they hid in a secret annex (hidden rooms). And we only know this whole remarkable story because a teenager named Anne Frank kept a diary. Let's read about this incredible girl.

Long before World War II began in 1939, the National Socialists (Nazis) led by Adolf Hitler took power in Germany. By 1933, the Nazis had started to make life bad for Jewish Germans, stopping people from going to Jewish businesses and burning books written by Jews. The Frank family, who were Jewish, saw what was happening around them in Germany and left for a better life in the Netherlands. Anne was just four years old.

Anne and her sister Margot, three years older, started new schools in Amsterdam, the Netherlands, in 1934. Anne's father, Otto, earned money managing businesses that sold pectin (a fruit jam ingredient) and then spices. Anne's mother, Edith, worked hard to set up their new home and look after the girls. Anne was a happy little girl — she liked books, movies and ice skating, and she talked a lot! She made lots of great friends in Amsterdam.

For a time the Franks escaped Germany's cruel treatment of Jews, but in 1939, the Second World War began, and in 1940, the Nazis took over the Netherlands. Though the Dutch (people from the Netherlands) tried to resist the Nazi's rules, the Germans brought lots of unfair new laws to Amsterdam: Jews could not own businesses or go to movies and had to attend their own schools. Some Jews were even arrested and taken to camps, where they died.

In 1942, Anne celebrated her 13th birthday with friends and a movie at home and got a wonderful gift, a diary covered in red and white plaid (cross-patterned). She called the diary "Kitty" and wrote to her like a close friend, someone that would keep her secrets and make her feel better. That turned out to be more true than she could have ever guessed.

Just a few weeks later, Margot was called to the German camps for Jews, as the opening to this chapter says. To keep Margot safe, the Franks had to hide — quickly. Fortunately, they'd been smart and planned for this. They had been gathering food and clothes and furniture to live in a hidden annex in the back of Otto's business building. There were three floors of small rooms through a secret bookcase. They planned to take cover there with another Jewish family, Hermann and Auguste van Pels, and their son, Peter, who was two years older than Anne. That night Anne packed her school bag including her diary, and first thing the next morning they went quietly through the rain to move into the annex.

Only six other people — employees at Otto's business and some of their family members — knew about the Franks and van Pels hiding in the annex. None of the other workers at the building knew. And they couldn't. If anyone else found out, these helpers and the Jewish people they were helping could be punished and maybe even killed. Their secret was a matter of life and death. So the Franks and van Pels never left the apartment. During the day, they kept quiet and walked in slippers. Every day their helpers would bring them food and newspapers and would come to chat during lunch when the other workers left to eat.

In many ways, the Franks tried to make life as normal as possible for their kids. They had school books and sit-down dinners. Otto tried to reassure Anne that the adults would handle the danger and the planning — her job was to keep living like a kid as much as she could. Anne was very close to her dad. For her part, she was incredibly positive. In the face of war and Nazi control, she wrote that still believed in the goodness of other people.

Anne was able to have many normal teenage feelings despite her hardships. She had a crush on her housemate, Peter van Pels, for a time. In her diary, Anne described how Peter's smiles and looks could suddenly make a dark day feel bright. She even had her first kiss with him. On the flipside, she was also terribly annoyed with Fritz Pfeffer, a man who later came to share the annex, and fought with him over who could use the table in their shared room.

After more than two years in hiding, on the morning of August 4, 1944, the bookcase swung open. Two policemen and a Nazi officer entered the apartment. The Franks had been found. All eight in hiding were arrested. Anne was sent as a prisoner to German concentration camps, where conditions were horrid. Forced into hard labor as just a young girl, Anne struggled to survive with little food or water and cramped, inhuman shelter. She got very sick. In early 1945, she and Margot both died. Their mom had also died earlier that year in a different camp — three victims among the six million Jews murdered in the Holocaust. Tragically they were killed just a few months before the Nazis surrendered, and the Nazi prisoners were freed.

Two of the six helpers were punished and sent to prison. All six helpers survived. Only one of the eight in the secret annex, Otto Frank, survived the war. One of the helpers who was not arrested saved Anne's incredible diary and gave it to Otto after the war. Otto spent the rest of his life sharing Anne's story.

Anne had actually dreamed of being a writer when she grew up. In her diary, she admitted that she wasn't sure if she could do it. Oh, but she did! Her diary had a bigger impact than she might have possibly imagined. Something about it captured readers across the globe — the honesty, clear writing and optimism of a young girl forced into hiding. Perhaps by sharing her ordinary life amid unreal horrors, she made the war more real to readers. Anne showed the lasting power that a young person's writing could have. Today, the annex is an excellent museum you can visit to see how Anne lived. Together with her diary, you can gain a small understanding of what an actual person — not just a name in a book — experienced in an unforgettable tragedy in history.

DISCUSSION GUIDE

Review Questions:

1. Why did the Franks leave Germany?

2. What event made them actually go into hiding in the annex

in Amsterdam?

3. How did the Franks get food and news while in hiding?

Discussion Questions:

1. How do you think Anne stayed so positive while in hiding?

2. What other ways do you think the Franks and other Jews tried to avoid the Nazis?

3. Why do you think the helpers decided to help the Franks? What would you do?

Project Idea:

Write your own diary entry. Anne's excellent writing has had a huge effect on millions of people. Think of a recent time you were in a new place, and write an entry about the place you were in and what it was like. Include a description and reaction to the place itself — a relative's or friend's house or a hotel. Then describe what you did. Anne included lots of detail about what people said and how she felt. A strong entry will do the same.

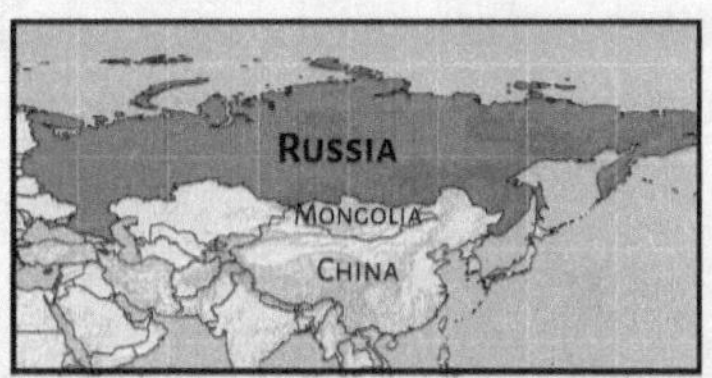

CHAPTER 25

RUSSIA: ANASTASIA ROMANOV (1901-1918)

THE LOST GRAND DUCHESS

The world wanted to solve this mystery: was Anastasia still alive? Her whole family had been killed when she was 17, and she had been with them. But no one could prove whether she was dead or alive. People really wanted to believe that she had survived. They hoped that the entire Russian royal family was not gone. What really happened to Anastasia, the youngest daughter of the last emperor of Russia? Read on to find out.

Russia had been ruled by tsars (pronounced *zars*) for nearly 350 years when Nicholas Romanov was crowned as the newest tsar in 1896. Nicholas was married to Alexandra, a princess from Germany. They had five children, the first four girls and then a boy, Alexei. The girls, born in this order, Olga, Tatiana, Maria and Anastasia, were called *grand duchesses*. They sometimes called themselves OTMA and signed notes that way — a name they created with the first letters of their names. Sounds like something you might do, right?

Growing up in the Alexander Palace near St. Petersburg, Anastasia and her sisters were not well-known personalities to the public outside palace walls. They were often photographed but always carefully dressed, usually in elegant white dresses, so that the Russian people assumed they were very formal. But the truth is, Anastasia was nothing like those pictures. She was not very graceful. She refused to sit still. She made everyone laugh. Legend says she once hid a frog in her tutor's desk!

And Anastasia had a strong will. She moved her little bed all over the palace to wherever she felt like sleeping — by the fire in the winter, by the windows in the summer and next to the Christmas tree during the holidays. She loved to carry a camera around and even tried to take a picture of herself in the mirror, maybe Russia's first *selfie*!

But while the Romanov girls lived a royal life, Nicholas and Alexandra's rule of Russia was troubled almost from the start. In 1905, Russian soldiers fought with protestors in St. Petersburg, leading to riots across the country. In response, Nicholas made reforms (changes) to the government, giving the people more of a say in their laws. But it was probably too late — most Russians were very poor farm workers who did not own land or even have modern basics such as furniture or running water. When Germany declared war on Russia at the beginning of World War I in 1914, the Russian people were left with even less. They began to fight each other, beginning with a revolution in February 1917.

The two sides fighting within Russia were the *Bolsheviks* and the *White Army*. The *Bolsheviks* were communists who said they would create a workers' paradise, where the government would run businesses and make sure everyone was cared for equally. The *White Army* was anti-Bolshevik, made up of some who supported the tsar and others who wanted a democracy, where people would vote on leaders and laws.

Anastasia kept her tough spirit in the face of this civil war. She even encouraged her older sisters to stay strong and not cry. But the tsar's side was losing, and some soldiers were even refusing to follow orders. So Tsar Nicholas gave up his throne in March 1917. He hoped that it would calm the country and let a new government bring back peace. Anastasia just wanted her dad to be safe with his family.

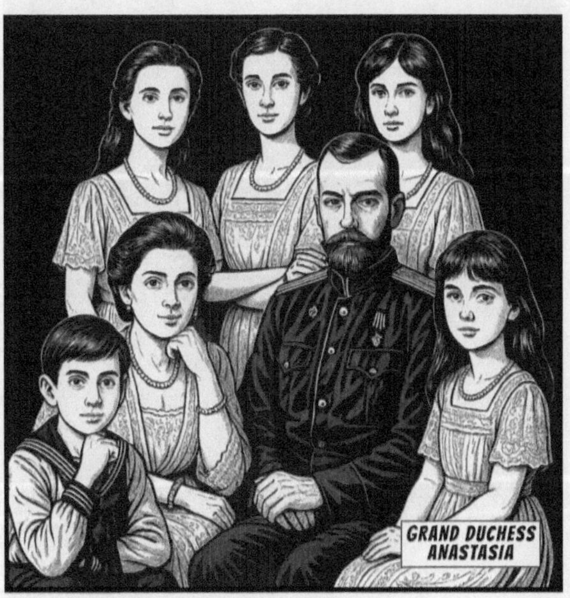

After Nicholas left the crown, Anastasia and her family were kept under guard, first in St. Petersburg and then moved to the middle of the country, far from the major cities. By spring 1918, the Bolsheviks guarded them as captives, awaiting the outcome of the civil war. Then, in July, with the White Army drawing near, the Bolsheviks got nervous that the tsar might be rescued and freed, so they killed him and his family.

Because the Bolsheviks were not sure how the country would react to the death of the royal family, at first they announced only Nicholas's death. This was before the Internet, of course, and communications were easier to control. Still, news leaked and people started to figure it out. But they didn't know exactly what happened, and many couldn't believe that the Bolsheviks would kill the whole family, including kids, 17-year-old Anastasia and her 13-year-old brother, Alexei.

Rumors began to spread: people said that Anastasia was still alive, that they had seen her on a train or on a crowded street. Most famously, in 1920, a woman in Germany was pulled from an icy river and claimed to be Anastasia. She spoke many languages and seemed to look like the young duchess. For years, she swore she was the lost Romanov girl until she died in 1984. True or not, Anastasia seemed to be the Romanov that folks kept alive in their hearts. Maybe because of that that woman's wild story. And maybe because Anastasia had been the charming, youngest princess...

The Bolshevik communists ultimately won the Russian Civil War. Over time, the Russian communists in many ways could be as ruthless as some tsars before them. They kept tight control over citizens' lives.

As a result, many Russians missed the old days. Anastasia represented a past that looked better to some.

The communist government broke apart in Russia decades later, in 1991, and people finally felt safe to come forward with information about what happened to the Romanovs. Later, with DNA testing (DNA is the unique map of each person's traits), authorities ultimately figured out what happened to Anastasia. Sadly, the story had a harsh ending. Anastasia had not escaped. She and the rest of her family and their servants were indeed killed in 1918.

Anastasia is included in this book not so much for what she did as for what her story can teach us. She shows us how brutal war can be, that even a young girl can be caught in the bloodshed. She also shows how much history changes depending on who is telling the story. That is, her tale was ignored by the communists. But memory of the funny, naughty duchess captured the imagination of the communists' enemies around the world. Books, TV shows and even a movie for kids were made about Anastasia. Those who wished she had survived told their own version of history.

DISCUSSION GUIDE

Review Questions:

1. How long had tsars ruled Russia?

2. Where the Romanovs' everyday home?

Discussion Questions:

1. Do you think it was smart of the tsar to give up his throne?

2. Why do you think the Bolsheviks didn't want people to know about the death of the tsar's family?

Project Idea:

Interview a Anastasia. Create a role-play in which you conduct an interview with a woman claiming to be Anastasia. Write a list of questions that you would ask to try to figure out if she really is the lost grand duchess. Where did she grow up? Who were her siblings? How did she escape from the Bolsheviks? Where has she been hiding? Why is she coming forward now? You get the idea! Then perform the interview in front of an audience and have them guess whether Anastasia is the real thing.

We have just covered a lot of ground! As we've traveled around the world and through 500-plus years in this book, we've gotten a real birds-eye view of history. With a broad look at many times and places, you can make some comparisons and think about some big questions. Let's talk about a few here as part of our conclusion.

How much has changed? In many ways, life was harsher centuries ago. People led shorter lives and faced tougher punishments. Lots of young children suffered from diseases with limited cures — many of our subjects were the lucky ones, but some, like Edward VI of England, died very young. Kids also had to grow up faster. They were forced to work, or in some cases to fight in wars, at a young age. It's hard to imagine being left to defend a fort at 14 like Madeleine de Vercheres in early French Canada.

How much is the same across time? In other ways, the human experience remains the same. People and nations struggle for power in much the same way now that they did long ago. Ismail I of Iran went into hiding to wait for his moment in the 1400s, sort of like José Martí did from Cuba in the 1800s. On the brighter side, people have always looked for beauty and knowledge. Michelangelo and Mozart passionately pursued their art and music and shared it with us. Savitribai Phule risked her own safety to teach the girls of India in the 1800s.

What about comparing different parts of the world? We saw similar things happen in different countries. Puyi, the last emperor of China, was used by others as a pawn in much the same way as Nicholas Romanov, the last tsar of Russia. Also, forcing religious changes was painful in both Iran and England in the 1500s.

What was different from what you expected? One thing I kind of knew that still surprised me in writing this book: castles in real life are really not settings for fairy tales. So much of the time we think of kings and queens and princesses as characters in stories that always have happy endings. In fact, the palaces were often built for defense and faced a lot of violence. And the lives of royals were often dangerous, ending tragically. Just look at Lady Jane Grey and Anastasia Romanov. I'm not saying that there aren't benefits to being king, just that fairy tales are just that, tales... What surprised you?

The Role of Kids. It seems that one constant across these diverse stories is the struggle for freedom. From Colombia to Korea, France to Ethiopia, so many important turning points in history come from people looking to free themselves from another nation's control. Kids have indeed played a role in these fights for liberty.

And kids have also brought so much pure joy to history. From Umm Kulthum, to Braille to Bombardier, this book is filled with young people who found passions, pursued them and changed the world at a young age.

Final Thoughts. Many thanks, truly, for joining me on this journey. I encourage you to dive deeper into any of these topics — there are longer biographies for many of these kids. Or if there was a time period or country you liked, there will certainly be more history to explore.

In closing, this book taken as a whole shows that even when looking way beyond recent (American) history we see that human nature seems to stay the same. That means that we all have more in common than we think, that we're part of a really long chain of events from all over. We can rest easier knowing that so many others like us have already been there. They may have worn clothes that look funny to us, but they probably felt a lot of the same things.

I hope my own kids take inspiration from the good and make better choices than the others, that they find the courage to follow their dreams and make a positive impact. Now we all have 25 more historic examples to draw from right here!

Most of all, I hope you keep reading, keep learning history, and keep stopping at those historical markers on the road! Thank you again!

Make History with Your Review!

"How far that little candle throws his beams! So shines a good deed in a weary world."
-William Shakespeare

You've just read about some incredible real-life kids who changed world history. Now you have the chance to help someone else find these inspiring stories!

Many people decide what to read based on reviews. That's where you come in!

> Your review could:
>
> ...help one more kid find his or her passion.
>
> ...help one more teacher find the perfect book for class.
>
> ...help one more family talk about a new story together.

Kindly consider leaving a review online – it should only take a moment, and it makes a huge difference.

Thank you sincerely for sharing the promise of kids and history!

N. H. Greenwood

Selected References (in Order of Use)

·France, A. (1909). *The life of Joan of Arc* (W. S. Whale, Trans.; Vols. 1–2). Project Gutenberg. (Original work published in French 1908–1909)

·Barrett, W. P. (Trans.). (1932). *The trial of Jeanne d'Arc* [English translation; with an essay by P. Champion, trans. C. Taylor & R. H. Kerr]. Fordham University, Internet History Sourcebooks. https://sourcebooks.web.fordham.edu/basis/joanofarc-trial.asp

·Nohl, L. (1880). *Life of Mozart* (J. J. Lalor, Trans.). Jansen, McClurg.

·Holmes, E. (1878). *The life of Mozart, including his correspondence* (New ed.; E. Prout, Ed.). Novello, Ewer & Co.

·Barman, R. J. (1999). *Citizen emperor: Pedro II and the making of Brazil, 1825–1891.* Stanford University Press.

·UNESCO. (n.d.). The Emperor's Collection: Brazilian and foreign photography in the nineteenth century. https://www.unesco.org/en/memory-world/lac/emperors-collection-brazilian-and-foreign-photography-nineteenth-century

·Massarella, L. (2016, September 7). Exclusive interview: Pele on his Santos years. *FourFourTwo.* https://www.fourfourtwo.com/features/exclusive-interview-pele-his-santos-years

·FIFA Museum. (2023, January 11). Pelé – a life in his own words. https://www.fifamuseum.com/en/explore/fifamuseumplus/blog/Pel--a-life-in-his-o

·Williams, R. (2022, December 29). Pelé radiated the quality of joy: An instant appeal to the eye and heart. *The Guardian.* https://www.theguardian.com/football/blog/2022/dec/29/pele-radiated-the-quality-of-joy-an-instant-appeal-to-the-eye-and-heart-brazil

·Fédération Internationale de Football Association. (2016, November 21). Behind the World Cup record:

Pelé. https://inside.fifa.com/tournaments/mens/worldcup/1958swe-den/news/behind-the-world-cup-record-pele-2852661

·Pelé. (2016, May 16). Letter to my younger self. *The Players' Tribune.* https://www.theplayerstribune.com/articles/pele-soccer-letter-to-my-younger-self

·Borman, T. (2022). *Crown & sceptre: A new history of the British monarchy, from William the Conqueror to Elizabeth II.* Atlantic Monthly Press.

·Tallis, N. (2016). *Crown of blood: The deadly inheritance of Lady Jane Grey.* Michael O'Mara Books.

·Shelley, M. W. (2013). *Frankenstein; Or, The Modern Prometheus.* Project Gutenberg. (Original work published 1831)

·Davis, L. E. (2012). Mary Anning: Princess of palaeontology and geological lioness. *The Compass: Earth Science Journal of Sigma Gamma Epsilon, 84*(1), Article 8. https://doi.org/10.62879/c20182498

·Natural History Museum. (n.d.). Mary Anning: The unsung hero of fossil discovery. https://www.nhm.ac.uk/discover/mary-anning-unsung-hero.html

·Taylor, M. A., & Benton, M. J. (2023). The life of Mary Anning, fossil collector of Lyme Regis: A contemporary biographical memoir by George Roberts. *Journal of the Geological Society, 180,* jgs2022-053. https://doi.org/10.1144/jgs2022-053

·Vachon, A. (2024, July). Jarret de Verchères, Marie-Madeleine (baptized Marie-Magdelaine) (Madeleine, Madelon) (Tarieu de La Pérade). In *Dictionary of Canadian Biography* (Vol. 3). University of Toronto/Université Laval. https://www.biographi.ca/en/bio/jarret_de_vercheres_marie_madeleine_3E.html (Original work published 1974)

·Museum of Ingenuity J. Armand Bombardier. (n.d.). Joseph-Armand Bombardier. https://museebombardier.com/en/joseph-armand-bombardier/

·Ingenium – Canada's Museums of Science and Innovation. (n.d.). *Joseph-Armand Bombardier.* https://ingeniumcanada.org/channel/articles/joseph-armand-bombardier

·Seagrave, S. (1992). *Dragon lady: The life and legend of the last empress of China*. Alfred A. Knopf.

·Puyi, A.-G. (1989). *From emperor to citizen: The autobiography of Aisin-Gioro Pu Yi* (W. J. F. Jenner, Trans.). Foreign Languages Press.

·Beech, H. (1999, September 27). The last emperor's humble occupation. *Time*. https://time.com/archive/6955501/the-last-emperors-humble-occupation/

· López, A. J. (2014). *José Martí: A revolutionary life*. Univ. of Texas Press.

·Martí, J. (2002). *Selected writings* (E. Allen, Ed. & Trans.; R. González Echevarría, Intro.). Penguin Classics.

·Library of Congress. (2025, August 25). José Martí. *World of 1898: International Perspectives on the Spanish-American War*. https://guides.loc.gov/world-of-1898/jose-marti

·Balcik, I., & Yildiz, G. (2025). Umm Kulthum (Ibrahim). *Fembio: Women's Biography Portal*. https://www.fembio.org/english/biography.php/woman/biography/umm-kulthum/

·Al-Bustan Seeds of Culture. (n.d.). Biography: "Star of the East" — The life of Umm Kulthum. *Umm Kulthum digital curriculum*. https://projects.albustanseeds.org/digital/kulthum/index.html

·Harvard Magazine. (1997, July 1). Umm Kulthum Ibrahim: Brief life of "the star of the East": 1904?–1975. https://www.harvard-magazine.com/1997/07/umm-kulthum-ibrahim

·TalkAfricana. (2024, January 5). Kebedech Seyoum: The fearless Ethiopian resistance fighter who fought against Italian occupation. https://talkafricana.com/kebedech-seyoum-the-fearless-ethiopian-resistance-fighter-who-fought-against-italian-occupation/

·Plaut, M. (2012, November 5). Ethiopian general who fought fascism: Jagama Kelo. *Martin Plaut*. https://martinplaut.com/2012/11/05/ethiopian-general-who-fought-fascism-jagama-kelo/

·Heller, R. (1979). Educating the blind in the age of enlightenment: Growing points of a social service. *Medical History, 23*(4), 392–403.

https://doi.org/10.1017/S0025727300052042

·American Foundation for the Blind. (n.d.). 200 years: The life and legacy of Louis Braille. https://afb.org/about-afb/history/online-museums/life-and-legacy-louis-braille

·Conway, L. (2022, April 14). New lessons in braille history. *NLS Music Notes* (*Library of Congress*). https://blogs.loc.gov/nls-music-notes/2022/04/new-lessons-in-braille-history/

·Winston Nicklin, M. (2025, July 24). How Louis Braille revolutionized a writing system—despite efforts to stop him. *National Geographic.* https://www.nationalgeographic.com/history/article/louis-braille-writing-system-creator

·Clarke, D. (2015). Blaise Pascal. In E. N. Zalta (Ed.), *The Stanford encyclopedia of philosophy* (Fall 2015 ed.). Metaphysics Research Lab, Stanford Univ. https://plato.stanford.edu/archives/fall2015/entries/pascal/

·O'Connor, J. J., & Robertson, E. F. (n.d.). Blaise Pascal. *MacTutor History of Mathematics Archive.* https://mathshistory.st-andrews.ac.uk/Biographies/Pascal/

·Maui Steel Guitar Festival. (n.d.). History of the Hawaiian steel guitar. Hawaii Institute for Music Enrichment and Learning Experiences. https://www.mauisteelguitarfestival.com/msgfhistory.html

·Shah, H. (2019, April 25). How the Hawaiian steel guitar changed American music. *Smithsonian Magazine.* https://www.smithsonianmag.com/smithsonian-institution/how-hawaiian-steel-guitar-changed-american-music-180972028/

·Soria, H. B. (2015, September 22). Joseph Kekuku. *EBSCO Research Starters: Biography.* https://www.ebsco.com/research-starters/biography/joseph-kekuku

·The Times of India. (2023, January 3). Savitribai Phule: The woman who started girls' school in 1848. https://timesofindia.indiatimes.com

·Bangalore Mirror. (2016, January 4). An amazing woman called Savitribai. https://bangaloremirror.indiatimes.com

·Khilnani, S. (2016). *Incarnations: A history of India in fifty lives.* Farrar,

Straus and Giroux.

· Symonds, J. A. (1893). *The life of Michelangelo Buonarroti* (Vols. 1–2). John C. Nimmo.

·Holroyd, C. (1903). *Michael Angelo Buonarroti.* Duckworth & Co.; Charles Scribner's Sons.

·Vasari, G. (1568/1912). *Lives of the most eminent painters, sculptors, and architects* (G. du C. de Vere, Trans.). Macmillan and Co.

·Savory, R. M., & Karamustafa, A. T. (1998). ESMĀʿĪL I ṢAFAWĪ. In E. Yarshater (Ed.), *Encyclopaedia Iranica* (Vol. 8, Fasc. 6, pp. 628–636). Encyclopaedia Iranica Foundation. https://www.iranicaonline.org/articles/esmail-i-safawi

·Halsall, P. (1998). The letters of Ottoman Sultan Selim I and Safavid Shah Ismail I. *Internet Modern History Sourcebook.* https://www1.udel.edu/History-old/figal/Hist104/assets/pdf/readings/02selimismail.pdf

·DiCicco, S., & Sasaki, M. (2020). *The complete story of Sadako Sasaki: And the thousand paper cranes.* Tuttle Publishing.

·Hiroshima Peace Culture Foundation. (n.d.). *Sadako and the atomic bombing.* Kids Peace Station Hiroshima. https://www.pcf.city.hiroshima.jp/kids/KPSE/sadako-abomb-e/sadako1945-e/sadako1945-e.html

·National Park Service. (2023, August 1). Origami cranes. https://www.nps.gov/articles/000/origami-cranes.htm

·Hiroshima City. (n.d.). Paper cranes and Children's Peace Monument. https://www.city.hiroshima.lg.jp/english/peace/1033408/1009685.html

·Hiroshima Peace Culture Foundation. (n.d.). *Did Sadako know she had leukemia?* Kids Peace Station Hiroshima. https://www.pcf.city.hiroshima.jp/kids/KPSE/sadako-abomb-e/subcon-e/more1955-e.html

·Moore, J. (2009). *Yu Gwan Sun and the March First Movement* [Lesson plan]. Western Kentucky University / The Korea Society.

·KBS World Radio. (2012, March 1). Yu Gwan-sun, the indomitable independence fighter. *KBS World Radio.*

·Cultural Heritage Administration of Korea. (n.d.). Historic site related to Yu Gwan-sun, Cheonan (Historic Site No. 230). Cultural Heritage Administration of Korea.

·Bayne, B. (2006). From saint to seeker: Teresa Urrea's search for a place of her own. Church History, 75(3), 611–631. https://doi.org/10.1017/S0009640700098668

·Holden, F. M. (2016, April 2). Urrea, Teresa. Handbook of Texas Online. Texas State Historical Association. https://www.tshaonline.org/handbook/entries/urrea-teresa

·Ramsey, R. (2021). Christ in Yaqui garb: Teresa Urrea's Christian theology and ethic. Religions, 12(2), 126. https://doi.org/10.3390/rel12020126

·Ruiz, V. L., & Sánchez Korrol, V. (Eds.). (2005). Latina legacies: Identity, biography, and community. Oxford University Press. https://doi.org/10.1093/oso/9780195153989.001.0001

·Anne Frank House. (n.d.). Anne Frank. https://www.annefrank.org/en/anne-frank/

·Frank, A. (1996). *The diary of a young girl: The definitive edition* (M. Pressler, Ed.; S. Massotty, Trans.). Vintage Books. (Original work published 1947)

·Metselaar, M., & van Ledden, P. (2018). *All about Anne.* Anne Frank House.

·Rappaport, H. (2014). *The Romanov sisters: The lost lives of the daughters of Nicholas and Alexandra.* St. Martin's Press.

·Fleming, C. (2014). *The family Romanov: Murder, rebellion, and the fall of imperial Russia.* Schwartz & Wade.

Abolition (outside U.S.): Mainly in the 1700s–1800s, many places (especially across Europe, the Caribbean, and the Americas) moved to end slavery and the slave trade. Campaigns, petitions, and new laws were a big part of it.

Addis Ababa: Ethiopia's capital city.

Algonquin: Native peoples in eastern Canada and the northeastern U.S. Also the name for a large family of related languages.

Allies (World War II): The countries that fought the Axis in World War II (1939–1945). It included the U.S., Britain, and the Soviet Union.

Ammonite: A long-ago sea creature with a curled shell. Today: usually a fossil.

Amsterdam: A major city in the Netherlands.

Atomic Bomb: A weapon powered by splitting atoms. Extremely powerful and capable of destroying a whole city.

Axis (World War II): The main Axis countries were Germany, Italy, and Japan. They fought against the Allies in WWII (1939–1945).

Beijing: China's capital city.

Bolsheviks: Russian revolutionaries and communists who took power in 1917 and won the Russian Civil War against the White Army.

Bolívar, Simón: A South American independence leader. He helped several countries break away from Spain.

Bologna, Italy: An old Italian city with a famous university and medieval buildings.

Boyacá: A region in Colombia and site of a major independence battle.

Brussels: Capital city of Belgium.

Cairo: Capital city of Egypt.

Capitalist: someone who believes people and businesses—not the government—should own and run most things.

Caspian Sea: The world's largest inland sea (more like a giant salt lake).

Between Europe and Asia.

Caste (India): A traditional social system that could shape people's jobs and how they were treated.

Catholic: A major branch of Christianity led by the Pope.

Chaldiran (Battle): A major battle in 1514 in which the Ottoman Empire defeated the Safavid Empire there.

Clavichord: A keyboard instrument played at home before pianos were popular.

Children's Peace Monument: A peace memorial in Hiroshima, Japan, honoring children and calling for peace.

Classics (Greek/Latin): The study of ancient Greece and Rome: languages, stories, and ideas.

Communism: A system where the government controls most property and businesses and says it will share among people equally.

Constitution (Written): A country's rules, written down. It explains how the government works.

Coprolites: Fossilized poop (yes, really). Useful to help scientists learn about animals' health and what they ate.

Democracy: People choose leaders and laws by voting.

Dictator: A ruler with huge power who isn't chosen in free, fair elections. Opposition isn't allowed much room.

Dimorphodon: A flying reptile from long ago (not a dinosaur) with a big head and sharp teeth.

DNA (and DNA testing): DNA is your body's tiny instruction code. Testing can show family connections and traits.

Dynasty: A ruling family line. Power passed down through relatives.

Emperor: A ruler of an empire, often over many different peoples and lands.

Empress: A woman emperor, or the wife of an emperor.

Enlightenment: A time (mostly in Europe) when thinkers pushed big ideas about reason, science, rights, and government.

Exile: Living away from home because you're forced to leave or because it isn't safe to stay.

Extinct: A kind of plant or animal that no longer exists anywhere on Earth.

Florence, Italy: A city in Italy famous for art and new ideas during the Renaissance.

Forbidden City: A huge palace complex in Beijing. Chinese emperors lived there for centuries.

Fossil: A preserved trace of ancient life. Bone, shell, or even a footprint — usually found in rock.

Genre: The "type" of story (or music). Mystery, fantasy, biography, adventure, and more.

Geometry: Math about shapes, angles, lines, and space.

Guerrillas: Fighters who rely on surprise and speed instead of big, formal battles.

Harpsichord: An old keyboard with a bright, twangy sound. Popular before the piano.

Haiti (independence from France): Haiti became independent after the Haitian Revolution (1791–1804). Africans and their descendants helped overthrow French rule.

Hawaii, Kingdom of: Hawaii when it was its own independent country with kings and queens (before it became part of the U.S.).

Hitler, Adolf: The Nazi leader of Germany. His actions helped start World War II and led to terrible crimes, including the Holocaust.

Holocaust: Nazi Germany's murder of six million Jewish people and millions of others during World War II.

Holy Roman Empire (Austria 1760s): A large group of European states ruled under an emperor. Austria was one of its most powerful parts in the 1700s.

Honolulu: Hawaii's biggest city and the state capital.

Horn of Africa: The northeast "point" of Africa. Ethiopia, Eritrea, Djibouti, and Somalia are there, forming a horn-like shape on a map.

Hundred Years' War: A long series of wars between England and France, stretching from the 1300s into the 1400s. Mostly about land in France and royal power.

Huron: Native peoples of the Great Lakes region. The term is also linked to a language group.

Ichthyosaur: A fast-swimming sea reptile from the age of dinosaurs.

Iroquois: Native nations in the northeastern U.S. and Canada known for strong alliances and political power.

Islam: A major world religion based on belief in one God and the teachings of the Prophet Muhammad.

Jurassic Period: Millions of years ago. A time of dinosaurs, plus many sea reptiles and other ancient animals.

Kimono: A traditional Japanese robe-like outfit. Often worn for special occasions.

Korean Declaration of Independence: A statement Koreans used to declare they wanted freedom from Japanese rule.

Lenin, Vladimir: A leader of the Russian Revolution who helped create the early Soviet communist government.

Latin America: Countries in the Americas where Spanish or Portuguese is widely spoken.

Loch Ness Monster: A famous legend about a "monster" said to live in a lake in Scotland. No solid proof (yet).

London, England: Capital of England and the United Kingdom.

Lord: A noble title. In the past, it often came with land and power.

Byron, Lord: A famous British poet from the 1800s.

de Medici, Lorenzo: A powerful leader in Florence who supported artists and helped the Renaissance thrive.

Lyme Regis, England: A seaside town in England known for cliffs full of fossils.

March First Movement: In 1919, a major, mostly peaceful protest movement in Korea calling for independence from Japan.

Mathematician: Someone who works with math to solve problems and figure things out.

Mexican (independence from Spain): 1810–1821. A struggle that ended Spanish rule in Mexico and made Mexico an independent country.

Mission/Missionary: A mission is religious work meant to spread a faith. A missionary is someone who travels to do that work.

Montreal: A large Canadian city in the province of Québec.

Mosque: A place where Muslims gather to pray.

Mount Maebong: A mountain near Cheonan, South Korea — a local landmark and hiking spot.

Mount Tambora: A volcano in Indonesia that erupted in 1815. The effects were felt around the world, even in weather.

Musket: An old-style long gun used before modern rifles.

Muslim: A person who follows Islam.

Nazi Party: Hitler's political party in Germany. It ruled as a dictatorship from 1933–1945 and was responsible for horrible events including the Holocaust and WWII in Europe.

Nile Delta: The wide, fertile area where the Nile River spreads out before it reaches the Mediterranean Sea.

New France: France's colonies in North America in the 1600s–1700s.

Novel (book): A long, made-up story. Fiction.

Occupation (by another country): When an army takes control of a place that isn't truly theirs.

Oahu: The Hawaiian island where Honolulu is located.

Opera: A story told through singing on a stage, with an orchestra playing the music. Usually dramatic with bold costumes.

Orchestra: A big group of musicians playing together. Strings, winds, brass, and percussion.

Orléans, France: A city on the Loire River. It shows up in big medieval history.

Ottoman Empire: A major empire based in what is now Turkey. It lasted for centuries (1299-1922).

Paris: France's capital and largest city. A center for art, revolutions, and big ideas for hundreds of years.

Pascaline: An early mechanical calculator. It could help with basic math.

Paleontology: The science of fossils and ancient life.

Patriots (non-U.S.): People who strongly support their homeland, especially during a fight for freedom or independence.

Persia: An older name for Iran, used often in history.

Philosophy: Big thinking about life: what's true, what's right, and how people should live.

Pilgrims (on a journey): People who travel a long distance for religious reasons, or to build a new life somewhere else.

Prodigy: A kid who's unusually talented and skilled for his or her age.

Professional: Someone who does a job for pay, often with training or special skills.

Protestant: A major branch of Christianity that began when some Christians in Europe broke away from the Roman Catholic Church.

Qur'an: Islam's holy book.

Radiation: Invisible energy that can spread through space. Some kinds are harmful to living things.

Renaissance: A rebirth in art, science, and learning that began in Italy and spread across Europe, approximately 1300s–1600s.

Rio de Janeiro: A large city in Brazil on the coast of the Atlantic Ocean.

Rome, Italy: Italy's capital city, famous for its Ancient Roman history.

Safavids: A powerful empire that ruled Persia (Iran) in the 1500s–1600s and fought major wars in the region.

Sari: A long cloth outfit worn by many women in South Asia. It's wrapped around the body and draped over one shoulder.

Seoul, Korea: Capital city of South Korea.

Shah: A king, especially in Persian (Iranian) history.

Shi'a Islam (Twelver Shi'a): A major branch of Islam. Twelver Shi'a Muslims believe in a line of twelve spiritual leaders called Imams.

Shirvan: A historical region near today's Azerbaijan.

Stockade: A defensive fence made from tall logs set upright.

St. Michael (Angel): An angel in Christian tradition often pictured as a protector and warrior.

St. Petersburg: A major Russian city near the Baltic Sea. Important in Russian history and culture.

Symphony: A long, big piece for orchestra. Usually in several movements—like chapters in music (fast, slow, then a strong finish).

Syringe: A tool used to push or pull liquid through a needle or small tube.

Ten Years' War (Cuba): 1868–1878. Cuban rebels fought Spanish rule for ten years (1868–1878). The war did not result in independence but helped lead to independence later.

Tower of London: A famous castle in London built nearly 1,000 years ago. Used over time as a fortress, palace, prison, and treasure storehouse.

Tuberculosis: A serious disease that often affects the lungs. It can spread through the air.

Ukulele: A small, guitar-like instrument with four strings, popular in Hawaii.

U.S. (independence from Britain): The American Revolution (1775–1783) was the war in which the colonies broke away from Britain and became the United States.

Urban: City-related. The opposite of rural (countryside).

Washington, D.C.: The capital of the United States.

White Army: Groups that fought against the Bolsheviks during the Russian Civil War.

World Cup: A major international soccer tournament held every four years, hosted in a different country.

World War I: 1914–1918. A huge war that began in Europe and pulled in many countries around the world.

World War II: 1939–1945. A global war fought mainly between the Axis and the Allies.

White Army: Groups that fought against the Bolsheviks during the Russian Civil War.

World Cup: A major international soccer tournament held every four years, hosted in a different country.

World War I: 1914–1918. A huge war that began in Europe and pulled in many countries around the world.

World War II: 1939–1945. A global war fought mainly between the Axis and the Allies.